# RETURN FROM EXILE

# Return *from* Exile

## ONE WOMAN'S JOURNEY
## BACK TO JUDAISM

*Carol Matzkin Orsborn*

CONTINUUM • NEW YORK

1998
The Continuum Publishing Company
370 Lexington Avenue
New York, NY 10017

Copyright © 1998 by Carol Matzkin Orsborn

Printed in the United States of America

*Library of Congress Cataloging-in-Publication Data*

Orsborn, Carol.
    Return from exile : one woman's journey back to Judaism / by Carol Matzkin Orsborn.
        p.    cm.
    ISBN 0-8264-1102-9
    1. Orsborn, Carol—Religion. 2. Judaism—United States 3. Jewish women—Religious life—United States. I. Title.
BM205.077    1998
296.7'15'092—dc21
[b]                                                                      98-18795
                                                                              CIP

Quotations from the Hebrew Scriptures are taken from *The Holy Scriptures,* published by the Jewish Publication Society of America (Philadelphia, 1917). Quotations from the New Testament are taken from *The New Oxford Annotated Bible, New Revised Standard Version,* edited by Bruce M. Metzger and Roland E. Murphy and published by Oxford University Press (New York, 1991). When quotations are cited by individuals other than the author, she has faithfully presented their version of the text, representing multiple unattributed versions of Scripture.

*To*

DAN ORSBORN

*my basheert*

To my agent, Patti Breitman

To my editor, Frank Oveis

To my children, Grant and Jody Orsborn

To my parents, Lloyd and Mae Matzkin

To my grandmothers, Rebecca Nemeroff and Sarah Matzkin

To my friends, Susan Kuner and Emily Askew

To my teachers and colleagues at Vanderbilt University

To my rabbis, including Abraham Joshua Heschel

To the Congregation Micah community

*You have my deepest gratitude and appreciation.*

# Contents

**PART TWO**
SECOND SEMESTER

# AUTHOR'S NOTE

This book is essentially a work of nonfiction.
The events, conversations, and individuals in the book
are representations of real events, with the following disclaimers.

1.  In order to protect the privacy of my peers,
the students' names are fictitious, and their stories
and profiles are composites of several individuals.

2.  The professors and rabbis' names, stories,
events, and conversations are real and accurate
to the best of my recollection.

3.  In order to provide an intellectual framework
for what transpired during my first year,
some of the classwork and events represented
actually took place during my second year.
However, the personal transitions I made
from exile back to Judaism took place
within the timeframe as described.

# PREFACE

## *Exile*

In spring of 1970, I walked up a dark, narrow stairway to my rabbi's office. Having parked down the street, before the one delicatessen in Glencoe, Illinois, my nostrils were still tingling with the fragrances of my childhood. Peppery pastrami, pickled herring, chopped chicken livers made with real schmaltz. The memories they brought with them, concentrated as they were in the walled stairwell, wavered uncertainly between delight and oppression. To watch me ascend, the curious onlooker would have wondered if I was a good kid who had gotten herself into real trouble.

I had. I had fallen in love and wanted to ask my rabbi for his blessing. The trouble was that I had fallen in love with a gentile. My fiancé Dan and I were the Jew and the gentile. I was the first in my extended family to fall in love across religious lines. But I felt sure that this rabbi, of all rabbis, would understand. Would know that God, my God as well as Dan's, had blessed this union.

The last time I had seen my rabbi had been shortly before I'd left home for college four years previously; and it was far on the other side of town, in a spectacular office overlooking Lake Michigan. At the time, our Reform temple, North Shore Congregation Israel, had just moved to its new home on a cliff overlooking the lake. From the outside, the startlingly white building appeared to transcend its glass and beam construction, thrusting toward heaven with aspiring self-confidence. Entering through its peaked arches, the mere human struggled against the vastness, footsteps echoing in the architecturally sanctified sanctuary.

I knew only one man who looked at home in this house of worship. Rabbi Edgar Siskin wore his black robes with monumental authority. And until my rabbi came to North Shore Congregation Israel, Rabbi Siskin was Judaism to me. I grew up in the shadow of his austere presence: a brilliant intellect who provided a sense of protection from the threatening images of the Holocaust that stole from my family's first television set. I do not remember ever seeing him laugh. But it was Rabbi Siskin, alone, who could stand at the bima of North Shore Congregation Israel and stay his own size.

My rabbi, the associate rabbi, was another story. He was one of us, round and fuzzy. Full of stories and songs. Secretly, my best friend and I called him Rabbi Bear, because he looked like the kind of teddy bear you might want to keep forever. On the High Holy Days, when Siskin opened the doors of the Ark, strangers would gasp at the sudden exposure of luminescent purple set against the pure white expanse. When Rabbi Bear opened the Ark before the members of my chattering confirmation class, we would giggle at the ostentation—but we did not hold him responsible. I felt sure Rabbi Bear would understand about Dan and me, for the rabbi and I had a special affinity for one another. Shortly before my graduation from high school, he had asked me to head up the summer program for returning college students. Grades alone would not have justified the responsibility, for despite my being a finalist in the National Merit Scholarship competition, I had regularly failed my Sunday school classes. My report cards reflected my resistance to the study of my people's history and religion, which seemed to me to be an endless parade of faraway places set amidst the social turmoil of disrespectful classmates who knew way too much about one another. I could not find the bridge between the texts and me. But Rabbi Bear saw something of my Jewish soul in my eyes—something that even as I sat before him above a dark stairway four years later, even as I planned to marry my gentile fiancé, I knew had not died.

I thought Rabbi Bear would understand about Dan and me because during that summer's program for returning college students, he encouraged me to follow my instincts fearlessly. I had big questions and unbounded curiosity. As removed as was my interest in Jewish history and culture, my passion for learning everything I could about meaning and purpose, life and death, self and other was strong. Spiritual yearning curled inside of my heart, kicking its feet with an urgency begging to be born. My rabbi gave me carte blanche. And so for one glorious summer, the world of my Judaism and the world outside the walls converged. Every Monday, stealing time away from my summer job as an intern reporter for the *Chicago Daily News*, I would get on the phone to invite spiritual leaders from the world's traditions to our Sunday morning college class. Ba'hai had their world headquarters on the North Shore. And the Theosophical Society was but one town away. Every Sunday, I would leave early in the morning, driving my mother's metallic green Mustang, from my manicured suburban dead-end street to the mysterious portals of ashrams and sanctuaries scattered throughout Chicago. I would carry my precious cargo back to the temple, holding tolerant and generous spiritual masters hostage to my round-trip questions. Never mind that only a handful of the hundreds of college students in our congregation would bother to show up, I was the richest person in the world, living in the spiritual center of the universe. This was my Judaism. Courageous and bold. A Judaism that believed in thinking freely, demanding answers of life, paying heed to the deepest behests of one's heart.

But this was not the only reason I thought Rabbi Bear would understand. For some time after I'd left home for the University of California at Berkeley, I received a letter from my best friend, one of the handful of faithfuls who had passed the summer with our beloved Rabbi Bear. Rabbi Siskin was retiring, she wrote, and the congregation was in turmoil. The temple fathers had gone outside of North Shore Congregation Israel to find his replacement. They had rejected Rabbi Bear for promotion. Because, she wrote, she'd heard that the people with power thought that *he looked too Jewish*.

Who knows what really goes on behind closed doors? Surely there was more to the story than this. But it wasn't only from my friend's letter that I heard this bitter, persistent rumor. Issues of class, of style, of authority, of ethnic identification, of religious, political, and social understanding came crashing together: Where was God in this situation? Where was justice? Just what does it mean to be Jewish? *Is it possible to be too Jewish?* Our rabbi had left, she wrote, taking with him the support of a portion of the congregation. While plans were afoot to establish him in his own temple, he was running his operation from a paper-covered desk in temporary digs near the town's only delicatessen. And before him now, sat a young woman who had traveled all the way from Berkeley, California, to Glencoe, Illinois, for one purpose only: to ask him for God's blessing. The God of Abraham and Isaac and Jacob, of Siskin and Bear, and of Carol and Dan.

Despite my failures in Sunday school, I thought I knew something about exile. Righteous Jews, devoted to God, forced out of their homes by hostile intruders. Set to wander through deserts and in strange lands. Rootless, yearning for arrival. Never quite feeling at home anywhere in the world. Vulnerable. Exposed. There is a rich tradition in Judaism of such exiles. Egypt, Babylonia, Diaspora.

For me, exile came not at the hands of my enemy, but with a single tear rolling down the face of my rabbi, my friend. Whatever Judaism was or was not, at that moment, it was no longer willing to embrace my journey through life. My rabbi would not bless our marriage. Neither would any rabbi he knew. Siskin had already made it clear that North Shore Congregation Israel was not a possibility. My descent down the stairway that led from Rabbi Bear's office was the initiation of my exile from the Judaism of my childhood, an exile that was to end suddenly twenty-four years later, and then only in the most unexpected of places and circumstances.

In the meantime, I left to tell Dan that we would have to seek God's blessing elsewhere.

# PART ONE

## 24 YEARS LATER

*First Semester*

# 1

# New Students' Luncheon

Vanderbilt University's Divinity School was a long way for me from the University of California at Berkeley, geographically as well as chronologically. And yet, as I opened the heavy door to the university building, I was swept within by twenty-four year old memories of the institutional hallways and classrooms of my college days. Why is it that places of learning have such a distinct aroma? Could the ink on posters offering used theological texts for sale in 1994 really smell just the same as hand-lettered flyers calling for a sit-in at People's Park in 1969? Even now, as I am on the verge of receiving my Masters of Theological Studies degree three years later, I find the atmosphere of the Divinity School building to be mysterious and eternal. It carries with it as much a tangible presence as the many students and professors who were soon to populate my life. But it is a mystery I now frequently take for granted, a portal to ancient times and a more perfect future that has become a living presence in my life. Back then, three years ago, I entered that building girding myself against the suspicion that these halls would change me in ways that I could not yet anticipate. After twenty-four years spending most of my days doing public relations for salami companies, hotels, and accounting firms, this was something deeply different—exciting and dangerous.

Even the name of my destination was challenging. "Refectory." Would the Christian students expect their dining hall to be named "refectory" in a way that was foreign to my world and experience? "Refectory" inspired images of raw wooden tables with hooded monks sipping their thin soup between prayers. I stood outside the door of the refectory, rehearsing my story one last time before plunging in. This was the new students' luncheon. Inside would be the people—my classmates, my professors, the dean, even the refectory workers—who would be my community for the next three years. Would they like me? Would I be accepted? Would I be the oldest person there? The only one not heading for the ministry? *The only Jew?* I was acutely aware that I had no special authority with these people. These were not my employees. They did not know that in addition to running a successful business, I was a well-respected author and lecturer. They did not know that I had been happily married to my husband, Dan, for twenty-four years, nor that I'd raised two terrific children now in grammar and high school. Most of all, they did not know that I was a Jew. Not with a name like "Orsborn." And I fully intended to keep it that way. It was none of their business what religion I'd been born into. Judaism was a long, long time ago for me. Since then, I'd dipped into many of the world's religions. If necessary, I'd dazzle my classmates with stories about mystics and saints of many times and eras. If the name of Jesus was to be invoked by someone at the head table, sanctifying this or any occasion, I would simply add him to my list of sufis and gurus. I would get what I needed from this place, stealing knowledge like a spy in the court of God, and get out and about my business again, new and improved—but with secret, dangerous places essentially untouched. While here, I would be invisible.

The chattering was cheerful and nervous, few eyes noticing me as I picked up my name tag and seating assignment, making my way to one of the long tables in the large room. Despite its fancy name, the room looked more like a cafeteria than a refectory. No monks. Today the refectory still looked like a cafeteria—but with white tablecloths and a head table.

I'd hoped to be seated with Professor Buttrick, one of the few faces I would recognize in the crowd. As I had considered applying to the Divinity School, I'd been invited to audit any course that caught my fancy. I'd chosen his course, a class on preaching the parables of the New Testament. Buttrick, in the tradition of Jesus, was a great storyteller. Parable by parable, he showed us how to approach the subject matter of the New Testament, seeing our way through two thousand years of historical and cultural lenses, to make an honest attempt to grapple with the original intent of the stories. Although the course had been designed for doctoral students pursuing the ministry, he'd welcomed me—albeit not fully understanding what I was doing there.

Some of what Buttrick said went over my head. But every once in a while I'd catch on to something fascinating. Like the parable of the mustard seed. In the Gospel of Luke's version, Jesus poses the rhetorical question: "What is the kingdom of God like? And to what shall I compare it? It is like a grain of mustard seed which a man took and sowed in his garden; and it grew and became a tree, and the birds of the air made nests in its branches." When Buttrick explicated the parable of the mustard seed to the class, he asked us to stop and think. Of course, when you hear the story, you imagine that from the tiny seed grew a mighty tree: tall, strong, and straight. It fits the contemporary ego to think of spirituality in grandiose images. But Buttrick pointed out to us that if you know anything about mustard—and the people of ancient Israel certainly did—it's that the mustard plant grows up to be anything but a giant tree. Certainly it is nothing like the cedars of Lebanon. It isn't even like the mighty oak. In fact, as Buttrick retold the parable, we could picture along with him the crowds at Jesus' feet roaring in laughter, knowing as they did that mustard is a rather nasty weed. As he went on to explain the theological implications of Jesus' reverence of the lowly, seen even in the detail of the nature of the seed he selected for his parable, I recognized in Buttrick the irreverence and free spirit of one who had been raised in the stew of New York's ethnic East Side circa 1930. Today, he was seated at the head table impossibly far away. I had no choice but to penetrate the unknown.

To the right of me sat a fragile young girl, her name tag aptly labeling her "Willow." To my left, Sammy, a ringer for Martin Short, but blind. Across from me, Jered, a red-faced young man with a broad Louisiana accent, who was speaking loudly to Mary, one of the more than a handful of older women—older even than me—I spotted happily munching on watercress and chicken salad as I surveyed the room.

"Hey, fellow camper, what brings you to the promontory of purgatory?"

Sammy turned in my direction. His eyes were shining white, and I, uncomfortable, wondered why he did not wear dark glasses to conceal his disability. But if this was the initiation of my adventure in earnest, so be it.

I chose my words carefully.

"I'm a writer. I write about spirituality in the workplace. Most of my education has been in Eastern philosophy—Zen, Hinduism, the I Ching. I tell stories from many of the world's traditions to illustrate my understanding of the universe. But there's a hole in my books. Having spent most of time studying Eastern philosophy, I do not feel comfortable with material from the Christian or Jewish traditions. I'm here to round out my education so that my books will have a wider marketing appeal."

"You're here for marketing purposes? Thank God. Everybody else here is so damn serious. They're all looking for God. Isn't that a hoot? Hey Willow, meet Carol. She's a writer!"

"Wonderful! I've always wanted to meet a writer!" The buzz around the table turned to my books. So I could still hold court, even here. I repeated my carefully rehearsed speech in all directions, north, south, east, and west—but even as I relished the attention, I knew that I was not telling the whole truth.

For I, too, was here to find God. And even more vulnerably, I was here to find God in community. The reality was, despite my accomplishments, despite my spirituality, I was lonely. And not just because we were newly arrived in Nashville, the heart of the Bible Belt, having followed Dan's dream of playing a role in the country music business. The truth is, I'd been lonely for most of my adult life. It didn't seem to matter how many friends I had, how many employees, how many books published and people attending my speeches and workshops—something was missing. When I closed my eyes and quieted my mind, I could often feel a mystical sense of unity with the universe. I felt whole and fully alive. But the moment I opened my eyes, the feeling dissipated. I longed for meaningful connection to others, for purpose and vitality. In retrospect, I believe that it is my finest quality—my saving grace—to have been willing to recognize and admit that an experience of God that could only be experienced on the mountaintop is not a full and mature relationship with the divine. I wanted the real thing, and I thought that I was willing to pay a price for it.

Polite applause rippled through the student body as Dean Fitzmier cleared his voice at the microphone.

"Let me begin my comments this morning with a greeting. On behalf of the faculty, staff, and students of the Divinity School, I extend to you a warm welcome. You have worked hard to get here, and we have worked hard to help you get here. And now that you are here, we want to offer you our best wishes on what we hope will be a most fulfilling and exciting chapter in your academic and religious lives. Last week, I had several opportunities to view you, not as I have for some months now, as individual applicants, but as an entering class. For some of you, the path to the Divinity School of Vanderbilt University has forced you to deal with boards of ordination and higher education—and that has meant that you have had to face questions of vocation and identity. Nearly all of you have had to count the cost of the Divinity School in a quite literal way: I daresay that en route to the school most of you met with a banker, financial planner, spouse, or partner to discuss the root of all evil—money. And most of you are still looking for a part-time job. For many of you, your theological education will also exact a high toll in terms of your personal relationships: your spouse, your partner, your children. While you enjoy the luxury of study and reflection, they will bear more than they otherwise might—and that sometimes produces anxiety, stress, and even guilt. What binds you together as a group is that it is costing you something to come to the Divinity School. I want you to know that we know this and we honor you for it. For our part, we promise to do all in our power to make your investment a worthwhile endeavor."

Buttrick shifted, his cane crashing to the floor. Sammy munched on his salad, loud smacks periodically interrupting the Dean's earnest delivery.

"At Vanderbilt Divinity School, you will be asked to examine your tradition critically and openly, to question your presuppositions, your languages, your theologies, your pieties, your self-understandings. There are times when you will be frightened when you should not be, complacent when you should. You must be willing to change the way you look at God, yourself, and life.

"Genuine critical reflection happens when you scrutinize your views and beliefs, when you subject them to the harsh acids of modern thought, and, having satisfied yourself that they are sound, adopt them with vigor and fortitude, knowing that they may propel you in new and unpredictable directions. I can put my personal goals for you this way: two or three or four years from now, when your name is called and you walk across the platform of Benton Chapel to receive your diploma, I want to be able to say to myself, '*There walks a theologian.*'"

As the Dean was concluding his remarks, his secretary began passing crisp, white class rosters around the room. The rosters floated toward me hand to hand, leaving nervous murmurs in their wake. *Costs would be paid. Would there be divorces? Nervous breakdowns? Unanticipated illness and the unanticipated burdens of anticipated debt? And worse? Which of us would emerge stronger for the challenges? Which of us would be broken?* Surely I would be one of the survivors, I told myself. I would gain the tools, the language, the stories to better argue my philosophy of life, emerging from the experience enriched by the community, the friendships—bolstered but not changed. My stomach, however, wasn't so sure.

When the roster finally made it to my plate, I quickly flipped the pages seeking out my name. Did they spell my last name right? Nobody ever sees the first "R." They got the "R." Did they give my business address or my home address? Home. All right. Which telephone number? The one I gave them. And then I saw it. The first indication that I was swimming in deeper waters than I'd anticipated. The final column: religious affiliation. In a long row of words beginning with "P" and "M" and "B," one "J." One "J" seemingly standing out on the page as if backlit in neon. One it's-nobody's-business "Jewish" flashing on and off before my eyes like an electric sign.

Carol Orsborn: Jewish. But it was just words on a page. How many people would make the connection that "Carol Orsborn: Jewish" was me?

# 2

## Coffee Hour

At the time, I did not know that I wasn't the only one who was upset at seeing his or her name classified by denomination. Having been in Nashville less than a year, I had little more than first impressions with which to compare the cultural and spiritual orientation of Nashville's religious life to that of my home of the past twenty-odd years, San Francisco. Clearly, based on my first months' experiences, I had moved to a spiritually foreign land. As Dan and I made our way into Nashville's business and social worlds, we soon discovered that the first question asked of us was not, as in San Francisco, "Where did you move here from?" but rather, "What church did you join?" To us, hailing as we did from a culture of consciousness trainings and meditation workshops, spiritual retreats and eclectic self-help therapies, we experienced the new question as intrusive—a too personal, not to mention completely presumptuous, violation of our privacy. If we responded that we did not belong to a church, our enthusiastic querants would enjoin us to try out their community of believers, each better than the next. If they pressed further, we would sometimes be forced to explain the circumstances of our interfaith marriage and the fact that we had blazed our own trail through the spiritual wilderness, a trail that transcended the limitations of any existing religious institution. But we soon learned we had to be very, very careful to whom we released news of our Jewish connection. Not, as I had feared, because we would wake up one day with a Star of David burned on our lawn. But because our newfound friends—should they hail from one of the many more evangelical churches in town—could hardly wait to share with us their Good

News. Once, having overshot our street on a dark, rainy night, I had turned around in the conservative Lutheran church parking lot a block from our home. A sign informed the congregants that upon their departure (not only Sundays, but also Wednesdays, Thursdays, and, from what I could observe, every day of the week), tanks freshly refueled with Bible Studies and Adult Learning, they were "entering the mission field." One Jewish convert was worth a hundred non-Jews, some evangelists were taught. And the way to us was not through anger or hatred—despite what we had done to their Lord—but to love us to death. Our children soon learned to consider their invitations carefully. At least one ice cream social sponsored by a local church group had climaxed with my son Grant's date on her knees, praising Jesus and praying for his salvation.

But at the same time we fended off our new neighbors' concern for our souls, we could not help but notice how enthusiastic most of these people were about their religious communities. Unlike most of our friends in San Francisco, they seemed to like going to church. Even the few Jews we had met felt strongly about their temples. They enjoyed each other's company. They could count on one another to help each other out. And their love of neighbor did overflow their sanctuary's walls. Even the clerks in the convenience stores, the workers in fast-food restaurants, the lawn service workers, and so on and on greeted us with such genuine friendliness that it took us several weeks before we stopped asking, "Do I know you from somewhere?" In San Francisco, we had become used to rudeness from the many service people we would encounter during our daily routines. In San Francisco, even our friends and neighbors—the people who we thought of as our community—had little time or motivation for the courteous interactions that were part of daily life in Nashville. The weekend before we'd moved, I was in desperate need of someone to watch my daughter Jody while I took care of last-minute errands. I know that my best friend would have loved to help out, but she was away at a spiritual retreat for the weekend, as she was most every weekend, and could not be reached. It seemed to me that everybody was at a workshop or seminar, improving themselves. While they were busy finding God, I was reduced to calling a baby-sitting service that put me out a cool $70 for the day.

I wanted a community, too, but not one that would force me to repress or deny any part of who I was and who I knew God to be. At least the Divinity School, attached as it was to a nondenominational mainstream university, promoted itself as a place to explore issues of religion and spirituality from an objective point of view. I had already discovered that there were atheists and agnostics in the school learning to read ancient texts and studying comparative religions for all kinds of secular purposes. There were future and current politicians and lawyers, professors and physicians, taking courses at the Divinity School, some less interested in furthering their relationship with God than in furthering their careers. Even the faculty was split between skeptical scholars and self-disciplined believers. If I didn't fully trust that the school had no particular religious agenda for me, I felt pretty sure that my personal relationship to God was strong enough to emerge intact from any challenge.

As the weeks passed since the New Students' Luncheon, the foreign territory of the Divinity School had begun taking on familiar shapes and forms. At first, I approached the informal conversation groupings that congregated in the hallways, in classrooms before and after sessions, and in the large, central common room, by steeling myself against the unknown. I had already discovered, to my relief, that people thought of me as the author, not the Jew. But just as importantly, as I began getting to know my classmates, I discovered that many of the students at Vanderbilt Divinity School considered their religion of origin, whatever the faith or denomination, to have become obsolete in their lives. Unlike the happy churchgoers outside our academic enclave, it turns out that many of them were at the Divinity School specifically because they wanted to sort through the debris of their traditions in order to salvage some vital relationship to God for themselves and their communities, not necessarily to buy the company line. During those first several weeks of classes, every conversation was like opening a surprise package. Willow's mother was Catholic, her father Methodist. They had compromised and raised Willow Episcopalian. But Willow was casually considering converting to Roman Catholicism. When she had seen "Episcopalian" in her denomination column on the class roster, she had fought the urge to stand up and ask the group to add a huge question mark.

Mary's friend, Joan, one of the older women, had been raised fundamentalist Baptist, and after playing a leadership role in the Twelve Step programs, was now a practicing Unitarian. She, too, had cringed at her public unveiling. Sammy had been categorized as Protestant but he was, in truth, an atheist. Of course there were classmates born and raised in the tradition of their mothers and fathers, who hoped and planned to become ministers in their faith, but even they questioned fundamental aspects of their religious institutions. Gays and blacks and women all had legitimate beefs. Mary was among several women at the school who had been told point-blank by their conservative denomination that the church fathers would not even consider giving them a church. Certain that ministry was her vocation, Mary entered the Divinity School on her own. She prayed daily that over the years it would take for her to get her degree God would melt the artificial barriers that kept her, and all women, from carrying out God's work in official paid capacities, confining them to baking cookies and volunteering to lead Sunday school classes for the children.

I admit I was surprised that the eclectic spiritual nature of my generation of seekers had penetrated the seminary walls. Having traveled the country promoting my books, I knew that there were plenty of individuals of many faiths and persuasions who were living their spiritual lives outside the boundaries of their childhood faiths— many, outside the lines of any formalized faith at all. My best friend in San Francisco had been a fallen-away Buddhist who was seriously engaged in a home-study program sponsored by Paramahansa Yogananda's "Self Realization Fellowship." She was married to a former Christian who had become a Sufi. Some of the people I met were at peace with their decision to leave behind childhood traditions to mix and match, to explore and to venture into new (or old) spiritual and religious territory. But many were unclear and uncertain about the twists and turns their spiritual lives had taken, with few roadsigns to help them navigate the milestones of life. How do people of mixed traditions find someone to perform their marriage? In what tradition do they raise their children? In which cemetery will they be buried? Where is God when you are fired from your job? Diagnosed with breast cancer? Faced with the residue of childhood admonitions and warnings concerning the ramifications of leaving the fold, there are those, perhaps the majority, who secretly wonder if their spiritual adventures, in fact, represent some kind of personal failure.

Emma was one of many rowing this particular boat. I had first spotted Emma across the common room, in deep conversation with Mary. We were at the first coffee hour of the semester, the Div School's once a week ritual, where students and professors chat informally over coffee, bagels, and doughnuts. I was still at the preliminary point of shyness where I felt I needed some excuse to meet people of interest. I liked Emma immediately because while I was still wearing dresses to school, she had already shed her stylish but middle-aged trappings for the blue jeans and T-shirts of our younger classmates. I made a mental note to buy myself a pair of jeans too. I nonchalantly wandered over toward Mary and Emma, hoping that once within their gravitational pull, they would invite me in. I didn't have to wait long.

"Mary's been telling me all about you," Emma said. "I've never met a writer before so when I heard you were in our class, I ran right over to the bookstore and read your latest book cover to cover. Right away, I knew you'd understand what I'm doing here."

"Oh yes?" I responded.

Emma was the first of many to share their life stories with me— one of the true pleasures of the Divinity School, to delve deeply into other people's spiritual lives upon first meeting. Emma had grown up in Kansas and raised in a fundamentalist Christian denomination. At seventeen, she explained, she'd fallen in love with a Roman Catholic, who'd agreed to give that faith up and marry her at her parents' church. The moment she and her husband had said their "I do's," they dropped out and did not trouble themselves with any religious conversation for fifteen years. Told that she could not bear children, they adopted a daughter. It was over the issue of baptism that they had their first religious arguments. "After fifteen years, he suddenly felt an urgent need to have his daughter baptized in the Catholic church." Emma had a surprisingly strong reaction against it. Despite the fact that both her parents had passed away, she found herself arguing for the baptism to take place at her childhood congregation. At one point, they discussed having the child baptized in both "with a Bar Mitzvah thrown in." That way the child would have all her bases covered. One godparent, witnessing the struggle, invited them to talk the situation over with her parish priest. Emma declined. The other godparent, an atheist, suggested that they were making a fuss over nothing. "Somehow, as the days unfolded, we just didn't do anything. We let it slip and never talked about it."

Things went along smoothly for a while. Their spiritual needs felt to them to be more or less handled by their shared conviction that "it is our job to live a good life, find comfort in our friends, and make sure the world is no worse for our having been here."

Then, unexpectedly, Emma found herself, in her late thirties, unaccountably defying her medical history of infertility by becoming pregnant and bearing a second daughter. Despite the fact that her spiritual life was virtually nonexistent, she thought of the birth as a miracle. Her husband dismissed her mystical musings by saying, "Emma, the truth is I knocked you up." But as her daughters grew through their toddler years and through grade school, the feeling continued to grow "that there's something out there—some force greater than ourselves acting in our lives. There's got to be more than that we are born, die, and that's the end. I don't know why religion has been a problem rather than a solution for me. Until now, I had no place to go for guidance. Everybody always seemed to have an agenda for me, that I buy into this or that program in its entirety. I finally figured out that there's either something wrong with me—or something wrong with the religions that have been part of my life."

The mystical feelings continued to grow, until Emma knew that answering the call to sort through her spiritual confusion was the most important thing in her life. Her marriage floundering, she had arranged for a year's trial separation from her husband, bringing the two preteen girls with her from California to Nashville as she paid the enormous cost of following her heart.

Emma's search for ordination in the conservative faith of her upbringing was her attempt at pulling herself out of a religious quagmire, her spiritual life creating for her many more problems than solutions. And Emma is far from alone, although statistics show that most of her peers—the baby boom generation—solve the problem not by confronting their faiths, as Emma was attempting to do, but by denying them. Wade Roof, author of *A Generation of Seekers*, reveals that religious drop-out rates among the baby boom generation were, by the mid-1990s, at an all-time high of 84 percent, The reasons for this are broad-ranging, with scholars proposing such explanations as that the emphasis on permissiveness in the child-rearing practices of the 1950s cultivated an emphasis on individual self-gratification over the traditional religious purview, self-sacrifice. Religious authority and practice, with its boundaries and demands, were replaced with a consumer-driven emphasis on personal fulfillment. At the same time, the dissemination of sacred texts across cultural and historical lines, made possible through archeological finds and new technologies, dissolved boundaries that had previously kept us isolated behind the walls of our separate faiths. Finally, there was the denial of a God who could allow such events as the Holocaust and the horrors of Vietnam, by many.

As Paul Knitter notes in his book *No Other Name*, "the religious history of mankind is taking as monumental a turn in our century as has the political or economic." Whether this turn will prove to be for better or for worse is yet to be seen. But I had the sense that it would be the task of people like Mary, Emma, and myself to do everything we could to set things right.

That I could even think the concept "Emma and myself" was big stuff for me, that first coffee hour. I was clearly not the only person in the room who felt estranged from the faith of his or her birth—sensing a relationship to infinite mystery while trapped in the finitude of human individuality.

Meanwhile, while Emma had been born a conservative Christian, and I had been born a liberal Jew, for the duration of our first coffee hour together it seemed that we were, indeed, rowing the same boat. I left the coffee hour euphoric, Emma and I making our way together down the hall to Professor Barr's mandatory course in Hebrew Scriptures, Hebrew Bible 2503, formally called "The Literature, Religion, and Faith of Ancient Israel." My euphoria, however, was not destined to last long.

# 3

# *Div 2503*

I was not in the habit of denying that I was Jewish. It's just that in the years between Rabbi Bear's decision not to marry Dan and me and some time in the midst of divinity school, I quite simply did not think that calling myself Jewish was an adequate or complete description of my religious, spiritual, or cultural life. When pressed, I preferred to introduce myself as someone who had been born Jewish, was married to a Christian, wrote books based primarily on Eastern philosophy, and was attending divinity school. The curiosity about other faiths and traditions that birthed in me that summer after high school had continued to grow through the 1960s onward. The bookstores in Berkeley were overflowing with newly released ancient texts holding the promise of peace and happiness. I bought as many as I could afford. Hare Krishnas danced blissfully on street corners, tempting us into their temples with sweet rice balls and lentil soup. Krishnamurti sat on pillows in the student union, surrounded by a sea of eager, young faces. Austerely dressed Zen practitioners sat next to me in class, taking their finals with a serenity that I longed to emulate. Posters offered t'ai chi; friends invited me to see Maharishi's meditators fly; stories were told of Indian mystics manifesting jewels out of thin air and sacred ash from their bare palms: I was living in a spiritual Disneyland.

Judaism was one rich voice in the spiritual choir. When Rabbi Shlomo Carlebach visited the campus, I worked myself into an ecstatic sweat dancing to the evocative Jewish tonalities that strike a chord with me so deep and true that I can only believe that they were programmed before birth into my genetic code. But while it was a Jewish offering, the dancers on either side of me were Christian and

Buddhist. When I came down with mononucleosis, my roommate gifted me with a copy of the ancient Chinese book, the I Ching. In the unreality of my low-grade fever, the esoteric text—accessed by the casting of antique bronzed coins—spoke to me as no other spiritual philosophy ever had. I began to cast the coins every morning, chanting along with a tape from Swami Muktananda in the late afternoons, and capping the day off with Buddhist meditation. At Berkeley in the late 1960s, we were all having trouble coloring inside the lines.

Some more than others. Recently I heard that my high school boyfriend's cousin, who came from a nice Jewish family on Chicago's North Shore, was the head of the Hare Krishnas internationally. There are so many Jews in leadership positions in Zen Buddhism, they have given themselves a name: Ju-Bu's. Open the pod of just about any spiritual group, be it meditation-based, philosophy-based, or holistic-practice-based, and chances are you will find Jews actively involved. My sense is that many Jews, even disenfranchised ones, continue to be deeply spiritual people. In fact, I have pondered the notion that perhaps those of us who got swept up in the commonalities of spirituality, mixing and matching practices and philosophies outside the traditional boundaries, have quite simply taken God at God's word. If God is one, after all—the Jewish watchword of our faith—then where could you go to worship that God would not be?

I did not believe that God was distinctly or uniquely Jewish. Rather I believed that God was God and that every tradition, faith, and religion were human constructions, based upon their interpretation of a particular piece of the truth. An experience of God is available to us all, but because our human capacities are so limited, we receive, channel, organize, and communicate our piece of the truth imperfectly. This is true not only for each of us, but it was also true for our spiritual predecessors upon whose understanding of the ultimate our religions are based. At some point during my divinity school career, I stumbled across William James's *The Varieties of Religious Experience*. James speaks for my intuitive understanding of spirituality when he explains that different religious formulations appeal to different types of people. There are psychological differences between the individual who would join an austere Calvinist prayer group, preaching a severe God who punishes transgressions, and one who would join a "new thought" congregation, in which God is lavishly experienced as pure love unfolding. So, too, there are differing spiritual potentials. Some individuals find meaning enough sleeping through Sunday morning services while others make the attempt to be consumed by the holy fire of God's presence. Did human beings appropriate their piece of the truth and adapt it to fit their psychological, cultural, and spiritual needs, preferences, and talents? Or did God send forth a billion unique manifestations of the divine in order to reach individual human beings in the way that would suit each one best? If we each have a piece of the truth, perhaps it is the human task to approach each other with our humble offerings. There is the mandate, among the teachings of many of the universalist mystics with whom I have passed the decades, to build together a sacred mosaic. One can only hope that this optimistic ambition finds its meaning in the unity of God, rather than the Tower of Babel.

And so it is that while I believed God to be greater than the human expressions of any religion, I intuited that Judaism had as much of a grasp of the truth as was possible for any tradition. But in the consumer mentality I brought to the spiritual marketplace, I wasn't sure if it was the one path that would serve me best: Was it a path big enough to contain my expansive spirit and intellect? Regardless, I was darn sure that anyone or anything I got involved with would be respectful of those for whom Judaism was the tradition of choice. Div 2503, "Literature, Religion, and Faith of Ancient Israel," was the first opportunity during my graduate career to put Vanderbilt to this test.

Every student who enters Vanderbilt Divinity School is required to endure the rigors of "LRF": the first semester concentrating on ancient Israel and the second on New Testament times. The classes unapologetically immerse new recruits in the tools and perspectives of modern scholarship. History, sociology, linguistics, literary criticism: All the disciplines from a broad array of social sciences are brought to bear on their understanding of ancient sacred texts and times. Who actually wrote what? Were there political and social forces at work behind the scenes? Hidden agendas that were anything but spiritual? What were the cultural influences on the stories and imagery? Were passages borrowed detail for detail from pagan mythology? Were the words the way they appear in our translations what was truly written in the original Hebrew text? If not, how and why were they changed? Which versions actually are the earliest? Were discrepancies between texts intentional or not? Is the way we understand and use the texts today the same way they were applied in their original cultural context? And what about the difficult passages that are never preached on because they are incomprehensible, boring, or theologically unacceptable to modern sensibilities? How does one explain, for example, Psalm 137:9: "Happy shall be he who takes your little ones and dashes them against the rock!" What are passages like this doing in our sacred texts? And, because they are there, what are we to make of them?

The results, particularly to those who entered the Div School with their childlike faith in their tradition's particular interpretation of the sacred story line intact, are not always pretty. Because Vanderbilt is known as a liberal divinity school and makes the attempt to educate and screen its prospective students during the application process, few arrive believing that the Bible was dictated by God word by word and that the versions that have come down to us today are free of human input, editing, and error. But there is a huge difference between suspecting that the lump in your beliefs should be looked at and actually enduring the process of diagnosis, surgery, and chemotherapy. Who would willingly volunteer to perform such a distressing but vital operation, to endure the pained expressions and burning questions from new students for whom every word could be a threat?

His name was James Barr, an elderly gentleman from Great Britain whose deferential demeanor belied the long list of impressive letters that trailed his name. Three times a week, for several weeks, he had rumpled to the podium of one of the school's larger classrooms to blast away our beliefs, in cadences more consistent with English tearooms than killing fields. Professor Barr was among the more famous and respected members of the faculty, holding a chair as Distinguished Professor of Hebrew Bible at Vanderbilt, having been the prestigious Regius Professor of Hebrew Emeritus at the University of Oxford. His real strength is linguistics, and he shared with us early on, with great relish, the story of a prized graduate student from Oxford who had just earned her doctorate by proving that the description of the color of Esau's hair is inaccurately translated as "red"; it was, she proposed, more of an orange.

Despite this foray into the obscure, Barr had easily convinced the majority of us of the power of words. As the only Jew in the class, and one of but a handful in the school overall, I took my seat daily, readying myself for combat should any hint of anything derogative against the Jews issue from his mouth. That day never came. Linguistics, it turns out, is a particularly useful scalpel for scraping away centuries of Christian liberties with the ecclesiastical traditions of interpretation that have hijacked numerous passages of Hebrew Scripture to serve theological agendas not intended by the original language. For example, the very first thing Barr said to us is that he would never refer to the sacred text as the "Old Testament." That, he explained, was a Christian designation that placed the sacred books in a secondary role to the "New Testament." Had these scriptures been superseded? Were they but a lengthy introduction to the real Bible, the one that tells the story of Jesus Christ? No, we were to study these texts as they were originally intended: as sacred texts that contain their own integrity. From this point on, we would refer to these sacred books only by their correct English name: the Hebrew Scriptures.

Over the years, Barr, through his many books and lectures, had become the foremost authority in the world at revealing the fallacies of fundamentalism. Fundamentalists, he explained, thought of the Bible as the source of complete, explicit, and literal truth. He saw his task as rescuing the original words and meaning from those who would appropriate them for their own purposes. In *Escaping from Fundamentalism*, Barr writes "that fundamentalism is not, as its adherents suppose, soundly founded upon the Bible itself. On the contrary, it is a particular tradition of interpretation, only one among several that can be reasonably maintained, and not by any means the most natural or the most faithful one."

Take, for example, the story of creation. Unless you have undertaken a careful reading of the Bible, chances are you have a fairly cogent feeling for how the story goes. You know that God created the world in seven days. During these seven days, the world is created first, then the living things, and finally man. Then out of Adam's rib comes Eve. But if you actually read the Bible, there's a big problem. The first few chapters of Genesis present two completely different stories of creation. In the first, toward the end of the seven days, after the earth and after the plants and animals, humanity is created "male and female" together, at the same time. In the second story, man comes first, made out of clay; then the earth is made fertile; only then are the animals created for him to name. Finally, in the second story, Eve is made out of his side to be his "helpmeet." Which is the real story? Man and woman together at the same time—after the animals? Or woman out of man's rib—the animals in between? Somehow, most of us have mixed them up together, picking and choosing the pieces that suit our logical minds or adopting the version our tradition taught us as children. While there is murkiness around the edges, at best, we think somehow it's our fault we've got it wrong, probably because we didn't pay enough attention in Sunday school. More often, however, we don't think about it at all. Because we are uneducated in how to read a biblical text critically, we are vulnerable to other people's interpretations, people who may well want to manipulate us for purposes other than what we would experience as divine, if we had the opportunity to know what the words in the scriptures really mean—and if we could think it through for ourselves.

Skipping ahead one story, take the issue of the exile of Adam and Eve from the Garden of Eden, known by Christians as the doctrine of Original Sin. Neither Christian nor Jew disputes that the story goes that Eve ate of the forbidden fruit off the tree of knowledge resulting in humanity's expulsion from Eden. But traditionally, Christianity has understood the expulsion of Adam and Eve to be an account of humanity's inherited sinfulness—the sin of rebellion—bringing down the punishment of death, redeemable only through salvation by the sacrifice of Jesus Christ. But a careful linguistic reading of the text reveals something very different. Professor Barr points out that neither the word "sin" nor "rebellion" appears anywhere in the Adam and Eve text. Neither is there anything in the story that implies that Adam and Eve were created immortal in the first place. If they were not created immortal in the first place, death would not be a punishment for their sins, but, as it is for all living things, their natural state. This brings us back around to the original Jewish understanding of the goodness of creation and God's uninterrupted love for God's creatures. According to Barr, in the Jewish tradition, with Eve's transgression, there is a sense of loss but not of a "fall." The implications of these differences in theological interpretations are enormous, impacting our divergent religious understandings from the broadest strokes to the finest details. Our deeply held beliefs determine how we respond to our children when they make a mistake; whether we feel that the world is a friendly or a hostile place; how we interpret pain and illness in our lives, and so on and on. Wouldn't it make sense to at least base our responses to these and many such important issues and points of view on the words and original understandings that were actually written in our sacred texts? And beyond this basic consideration, wouldn't it make sense to submit our fondest theological notions to the scrutiny of all the tools, traditions, and disciplines that are at our disposal? Didn't God create us with rational minds as well as faithful hearts? Are we betraying God—or serving God—when we access the full range of our gifts, skills, and potential, including our intellects, to seek to deepen our understanding and relationship to God?

Having grown up in a liberal Jewish tradition, I was raised in a culture that placed a high premium on thinking for one's self. Even among the Orthodox, the rabbinical approach to study of ancient texts was one of challenge, questioning, and debate—rather than placid acceptance of doctrine. As I watched Barr's mind at work, I came to trust that the application of rational thought to the sacred text of the Jewish people could only turn out for the best.

But while Barr's mind brilliantly wove in and out of the Hebrew Scriptures, blasting away layers of misinterpretation to expose the vitality of the original text, his interpersonal skills with his students suffered from the very same British reserve and tact that makes him such a charming man outside the classroom. On the very first day he set a policy of taking no student questions, preferring to perform his surgery without interruption. His hope was that we would save up all of our internal combustion to release at our once-a-week sessions with his hardworking teaching assistants. We would not be deterred, however. So tentatively at first, then with gently accelerating intensity, the class was developing a technique to make itself heard. The technique was this: wait for Barr to take a breath, then shoot up your hand and start talking all at the same time, usually without being recognized.

This class, like all my classes, had its talkers—individuals who could be counted on to voice their questions, feelings, and opinions. It was often the same four or five people, ranging from ill-informed and obnoxious to highly sophisticated and insightful. Sammy was a talker, taking every opportunity to relate the lecture material to issues of disability. He began piping up during the discussion of Jacob's deceit of the aged and blind Isaac, in which Jacob takes advantage of his father's disability to steal his father's blessing from Esau. Sammy unceremoniously interrupted Barr, who had spun out into some more discussion about the color red (Esau is described as red and hairy), following the scarlet thread into the dish of red lentils that for some unfathomable reason plays a key role in the Jacob–Esau saga.

In the midst of Barr's scholarly discourses, Sammy's questions often took on the tone of a political debate, questioning the implications of the story's message in terms of current public policy. Barr, reluctantly ceding the floor, would pause politely until whoever it was that was raising their particular issue had finished. If the answer could be related to linguistics, Barr would be gracious and brief in his response, returning as quickly as possible to the lecture material. If it could not, Barr would simply thank the person for their question as a formal courtesy and move on without any other response. At these times, it was unclear as to whether he had actually listened to the question or had passed the time thinking about how many variations of this color or that appeared in any particular passage.

Willow, despite her serene demeanor, was a talker. Her quiet questions often inspired Barr to reveal deeper layers of the material than would otherwise have been exposed. I never minded when Willow interrupted Barr.

And then there was Jered. After a while, every time Jered would interrupt Barr, Emma's and my eyes would meet in a moment of spontaneous sympathy for what Barr would soon endure. Jered, the preacher from Louisiana, was one of the few people in our class who believed that the scriptures had been dictated by God word by word. What he was doing at Vanderbilt was a deep mystery to me. There were rumors that he had been sent to spy on behalf of the real Christians from inside the devil's own camp. I don't know which I minded more, his time-consuming, illogical, and ill-informed rebuttals of Barr's historical and linguistic testimony, or the way he would always speak up "on behalf of his people." "What you say may make a lot of sense up here in this ivory tower, but how will it play in the pews?" was his theme song. Barr would thank him and we would move on as quickly as possible.

Despite the presence of people like Jered in the class, by the third week of school, I had relaxed considerably. I was beginning to make friends and get the feel for being back in class after twenty-four years. Despite the many questions that popped into my mind as Barr talked, I remained uncharacteristically silent. I still didn't want to attract any attention to myself as the only Jew in the class. In fact, I planned to keep it that way throughout my three years in the Divinity School. After all, I was just starting to get comfortable in the community. It was such a pleasure to be just one of the gang, a member of the class with no special powers or privileges. But on the third week, as we continued our study of Abraham, Barr began class by reading the passage in Genesis in which Abraham, upon arriving in Egypt, passed off his wife, Sarah, as his sister in order to protect his own life. While the subterfuge worked, it came at the cost of Sarah having to spend some time in the Pharaoh's harem doing who knows what with who knows whom.

Jered could not contain himself, not even waiting to raise his hand. In a hoarse stage whisper, unfortunately clearly heard by most of the students around him, including me, he muttered: "That's why we needed Christianity: to redeem the morally bankrupt Hebrews."

Not satisfied with his small audience, Jered's hand shot up as Barr reluctantly acknowledged the interruption. "The problem with Abraham is that his behavior is unethical by the standards of the New Testament . . ."

It was apparent that Jered was just getting started but Barr wasted no time. As soon as Jered took his first breath, he dismissed the comment with a perfunctory "thank you" and continued on.

Nobody said a word. I waited. I looked at Willow and Emma and Mary. They had clearly heard Jered's first as well as second remarks. Their heads were bent down, taking the moment of quiet to fill in their notes. Barr picked up on his lecture theme as if nothing had happened. But I sat near the back of the room, my habitual seat, stomach and head swirling. Could I let this pass? *No. I could not.* I raised my hand and began to speak. My voice was quavering but loud as I asked the group if they had heard what had just been said.

"I'm a Jew," the words came pouring out. "And I'm deeply offended by Jered's comments. The Hebrew people do not need to be redeemed. Jewish moral standards are no less ethical than Christian ones. And what's more, it's bad enough that Jered said it. But where are all of you? Is there no one in this room who feels it necessary to respond to Jered's comment?"

The class was close to ending, but I am not sure what happened in those next few moments. I only know that I had never felt so exposed in my life. It was as if an ancient cloud of fear and anger enveloped me, separating me from all others in the room. Inside of it, I wondered if the ride was over for me so soon at Vanderbilt, if I would now be shunned by my classmates. Perhaps I owed it to myself to drop out. The thought saddened me, for since coming to Vanderbilt, I had been the happiest I'd been in years. I loved the growing camaraderie during coffee hours and classroom discussions. I relished my time in the library, culling gems from ancient texts. I looked forward with such anticipation to my exchanges with Professor Buttrick. But if this meant that it was over for me, so be it. I know what it feels like to have an illusion cracked. It's painful for a while—but the very place where the break occurs is the very place that my character and spirit would grow back strongest. I surrendered to destiny, whatever the future might bring.

At last the class was over and Barr left the room quickly. Many students milled around. But still, nothing more was said. I gathered up my books, feeling completely alone. But the feeling was not to last long, for before I'd even finished zipping up my backpack, I looked up to see a dozen classmates heading toward my desk.

Willow got to me first.

"Oh my God, Carol. You are so right! I'm so ashamed of myself. I heard exactly what Jered said and I simply dismissed it as just more Jered. But that was so wrong. Please forgive me! It will never happen again." She looked as if she wanted to go on, to say something more to me. But before she could, several other classmates came forward to shake my hand, to embrace me, to communicate their support in every one of a dozen ways.

"Go get 'em!" Sammy shouted out to me, waving his cane around his head as he left the room.

I had been revealed and I had survived. I put aside my thoughts of dropping out, for the moment. But in the back of my mind, I knew that this was not the end of this matter. It was only the beginning.

# 4

# Buttrick's Class

Each class that enters the Divinity School has a defining moment that determines the character and nature of the time it will spend together. My impassioned speech was our moment. For better or for worse, for those of us receptive to such raw exchanges, the incident served to peel layers off our façades. Despite the warmth of our casual and classroom exchanges prior to the Abraham crisis, I had not been the only one who had been hiding. Clearly, the challanges to the status quo that Dean Fitzmier had told us about at our opening luncheon were beginning. From that day on, the class quickened in sorting itself out into informal groupings divided along fluid edges.

All kinds of classmates I'd never even particularly noticed before suddenly became a big part of my days. They were the ones who had thought that I'd shown courage and inspiration in speaking my mind. Some had felt shame for their own quiescence, others had felt admiration for my willingness to speak my truth out loud. Some of them had never known a Jew before and were excited to have the opportunity to ask questions of me. Carlton was in this camp.

Carlton was aiming for a job as a chaplain in the army reserves. He, too, came from a conservative congregation in rural Louisiana. But he could not have been more different from Jered. Carlton, in his simple forthright way, wanted to be the best chaplain the army reserves had ever had. One thing concerned him. He knew that in the reserves, military chaplains could be called on to minister to people of any faith. His mentor, a Disciples of Christ minister from Kentucky, he told me, had been stationed across the ocean in a remote outpost during the Korean War. There were three Jews stationed with him and they had come to him one spring to ask him if he could help them do a Passover Seder. The minister had been so intent on helping them, he had even negotiated the purchase of a lamb from the village nearby. He had a Haggadah, along with do-it-yourself instructions, air-expressed to him from a rabbi friend he'd kept from his college days.

"Can you teach me the prayer over wine?" Carlton asked me.

I suppose I could piece it back together. The prayers over wine and bread, the Sh'ma, I still had those key pieces stored in my memory bank.

But sometimes he would ask me questions that showed me how much I, let alone my Christian classmates, had to learn.

"Do you take a ritual bath every month? I heard that Jewish women need to do that after their periods. What will I do for the wives of the soldiers? Will any bath do? Are there special salts to put in the tub? Prayers?"

I patiently explained to Carlton the difference between Orthodox and Reform Jews, and that not only did I not do mikvahs routinely, but that I had never done one. In fact, I wasn't at all sure what it was all about and whether people did still indulge in such ancient rituals; certainly, the Reform Jews I knew did not.

He looked crestfallen. Carlton was among many of my classmates who had a romanticized notion of Judaism as a highly ritualized community of believers, separated from the mainstream of society by special laws, practices, and dress. Despite my obviously inadequate explanations and personal demurrals, I was nevertheless enthroned as the informal class expert on all matters Jewish. Since we were all in the Hebrew Scriptures boat together, there were many opportunities for questions related to Jewish issues to arise among my Christian classmates, and so it was that I was never alone at a coffee hour again, looking for an excuse to break into a conversation. I did the best I could with their questions. But it became increasingly and alarmingly clear to me that despite my inborn cultural and social understandings of Reform Judaism—along with some rudimentary liturgical issues viewed mostly from a child's perspective—many of my classmates had learned more about formal aspects of Judaism in their college-level religion classes than I had in twelve years of Sunday school classes.

My growing circle of friends was not the only group that had found each other that day, however. Another, thankfully much

smaller group, had been founded pretty much on their shared opinion that I was an emotion-fueled troublemaker. They were not part of
Jered's tiny circle, who didn't so much want to avoid me as to convert
me. The group who thought of me as trouble tended to include the
younger, career-minded students who just wanted to get through this
program, get their degree and ordination, and start making a living as
quickly as possible. Their friendship group rapidly developed beyond
reaction to me. In fact, I was soon forgotten as the dialogue in their
circle moved on to more important matters, such as which denominations had the best salary packages, which ones allowed you to
choose your ministerial placements rather than being assigned, which
offered the best parsonages, and the like. As the year progressed and
the challenges to their placid approach came not only from my quar-
ter—but from all quarters—their boundaries began to melt, and the
groups began to flow more naturally from one to another. Still, it
quickly became pretty obvious who was friends with whom, and
what the nature of the discussion was likely to be when they gathered
together in the common room.

In the midst of all this activity, I looked forward to my weekly
class with Professor Buttrick, a doctoral level course on Christian
Apologetics that I had received special permission to join. The class
was important to me, not only because I knew I would get to spend
some time basking in the grounded presence of my favorite professor
but also because I was doing so in the company of the doctoral students. If professors are kings and queens of the Div School world, the
doctoral students are the inner circle of the royal court. Even though
many of them were younger than me, they carried themselves with an
air of authority that caused me to think of them respectfully as my
elders. They knew things and did things that seemed way beyond
anything and anyone I had ever known. In casual conversation they
would let drop that they had just returned from England where they
had studied ancient Phoenician in order to better understand the culture and heritage of Jezebel. They went on archaeological digs in
Israel. They threw off words like "rhetorical criticism," "phenome-
nology," and "hermeneutics of feminism" without apology or hesita-
tion. Many of them would be my discussion leaders over the coming
years, as preceptors and assistants to their mentoring professors. But

for now, in this doctoral level course, I was part of their community. There would, at least, be no one even remotely like Jered in this room. In fact, this particular course on Christian Apologetics was designed, as were many of Buttrick's courses, specifically to address such misappropriations of the Christian message and to reclaim the spirit and sense of what Christianity in particular—and religions in general—could be when at their best, not their worst.

And so it was to this refuge of scholarly sophistication, presided over by a man I knew to have a good heart, that I fled after my defense of Abraham, my integrity, and the Jewish people.

I got to class early and even so, in the tiny world of Vanderbilt Divinity School, Buttrick had already heard what had happened. In fact, he was talking it over with one of his prize students, Lester, a robust black man, who was to become one of my special divinity school buddies. "It's the Marcionite heresy," Lester was saying to Buttrick, who was nodding approvingly even as I walked in the door.

"Carol! Join us. Are you all right?"

I set my books down and pulled up a chair. While I already understood that I would not be shunned either for my public protest nor for my Jewish heritage by the Div School mainstream, I was yet at a loss for how to hold the incident that had occurred. Was what Jered had said about the Hebrew Scriptures needing redemption his own thing? A common thought among Christians? And further, and even more threatening in some ways, how did I personally feel about Abraham's willingness to pass his wife off to the Pharaoh's harem in order to save his own life? Abraham was one of the Jewish patriarchs. Was he also a liar and an opportunist? I preferred my saints, mystics, and gurus to be above reproach: transcended and transmuted. Why did religion have to be such a messy affair?

"The Marcionite heresy," Buttrick explained. "Back in the middle of the second century, a Christian scholar by the name of Marcion set himself to the task of assembling the first-known collection of Paul's letters. The thing is, Marcion was condemned as a heretic because of his own thoughts and contentions about the relationship between the Hebrew Scriptures and the New Testament. In brief, he believed that the God of the Hebrew Scriptures was not the father of Jesus Christ. He thought of the God of the Old Testament as morally limited.

Then he denied the goodness of creation. It's a point of view that unhappily bubbles up from time to time through Christian history. But even at our worst, I should point out that Marcion was condemned as a heretic. After all, think about it: The Bible that Jesus, himself, thought of as sacred text . . . what was the only Bible in existence during his lifetime? The New Testament obviously had not been written yet. When Jesus read scripture at a worship service, when he quoted passages, when he expressed his moral and spiritual points of view—what was his source? The Hebrew Scriptures. And where does the Christian understanding of creation come from? Or the Ten Commandments? Of course Marcion was condemned. And anyone else who would dare to put forth such an evil and erroneous notion—they ought to be condemned, as well!"

This was to be the first of many discussions I would have over the years with Buttrick concerning the relationship of the Hebrew Scriptures to Christianity. Buttrick has gone way out on some very public limbs to declare that everything that Jesus thought, spoke, and lived was not only consistent with but also came out of what he had learned from the Hebrew Scriptures. It isn't only his advanced age, nor his dramatically wielded cane—equalled only around the Div School by Sammy's flourishes—that gives Buttrick the courage to stand up for what he believes to be true and right. Buttrick is what I call a man of God. He sees through the superficialities of so much of contemporary religion: consumer-driven churches and synagogues that have replaced the powerful prophetic center of our religious traditions with ineffectual social institutions that largely are more concerned about business networking and social activities, about making life as pleasant and easy as possible—rather than about the hard and challenging work of loving one's neighbor, the true task to which we have all been called.

Buttrick views Jesus as part of the prophetic and rabbinical traditions in Judaism, using the spiritual and ethical tools he had gained from his serious study of the Hebrew Scriptures in order to do what any prophet worth his salt would: make sure that his people, the Jews—and any others whom he could convince to embrace his God, the God of Abraham—really walked their talk. But Buttrick soundly rejected that the New Testament itself provided anything essentially different or additional to the living out of a full and good life as the God of the Hebrew Scriptures intended it for God's people.

I felt comforted by Professor Buttrick's and Lester's assurances. But even this moment of stability was not to last. As the class was filing into the room, Buttrick presented to me what he thought were two great gifts. Each of us in this class had the assignment of writing a sermon on a passage of scripture. Rather than write on the assigned subject matter—any of the parables of Jesus—I could pick one of the stories from Hebrew Scripture. In fact, from this point on, he suggested to me before the assembled group, I was to replace any of his New Testament or church-based projects with my own religion's traditions and texts. For example, if he asked the class to write about the meaning of Eucharist, I was to take on instead the meaning of Passover. Instead of analyzing how church doctrine translated into liturgical forms, I was to look at the historical and theological roots of the Jewish Sabbath service. This was the first gift.

The second gift was the suggestion to seek out the professor of New Testament studies who had come to Vanderbilt Divinity School at the beginning of the very same semester I had. I was to tell her about our conversation and about my concerns and fears. Why the professor of New Testament studies? Because she, too, was Jewish. I was given the Buttrickian mandate to go talk to Professor A.-J. Levine.

The class proceeded and from what filtered in through my busy mind and beleaguered heart, it was as fascinating a discussion as usual. But I felt that I had somehow slipped from the frying pan and into the fire. I had successfully fended off the Marcionite heresy, at least for the time being. My continued attendance at the Divinity School was assured. But now I had the sinking feeling that I had been deeply misunderstood. Was I now to be pegged in every corner of this place as The Jew? I didn't come here to get passed off to the handful of Jewish faculty for special treatment. All I wanted was a place to go every day where I could talk with other people about my favorite topics, God and religion—and maybe pick up a few good Christian and Jewish anecdotes for my books. Instead, life was spinning out of my control.

# 5

## *Seeds on Rock*

I decided to defy Buttrick's good ideas for me, refusing to be pigeonholed. Believing as I did that at the heart of all of our religions could be found the universal experience of divine truth as I had come to intuit it, I set out for the Divinity School library. My sacred task was to begin research on the Jesus parable I had privately selected for my first attempt at biblical exegesis: the scholarly effort to place a particular passage of text into historical, cultural, theological, and/or literary context. The shelves of the reference room were filled with books, some of them containing as many as ten or fifteen volumes within a single collection, that did nothing but analyze each and every word, sentence, paragraph, and passage of both the Hebrew Scriptures and the New Testament in spectacular detail. In some cases, a single author would explain his or her point of view. In others, the best or at least most notorious thinking of a broad range of scholars from across the continuum of time, as well as disciplines and persuasions, would be revealed. The debates as well as the agreements, the quirks and the mainstream opinion were all represented, providing entry into the innermost sanctum of thoughts about these sacred texts. For someone who had spent most of her life in search of deeper meaning and hidden knowledge this was sheer heaven.

The Divinity School library had already proven itself to be my favorite haven. In particular, it had become my habit to spend many hours making my way through the large bright red paperback collegiate edition of *The New Oxford Annotated Bible with the Apocrypha: An Ecumenical Study Bible,* completely revised and enlarged, as I sat comfortably in one of the reference room's two overstuffed tweedy pink chairs. When I came to a passage that troubled or confused me—Genesis' mighty race of giants, born of angels mating with human women only to be presumably wiped out in Noah's flood, for example—I'd pop up and look it up in one of the big volumes. Sometimes I'd venture through the connecting door into the school's extensive Jewish library—one of the largest in America, having been recently expanded through a gift by a local Jewish family. I knew the Jewish library was there. In fact it had been an important symbol to me that the school was giving me more than lip-service when the admissions director assured me how welcome I would be. But unlike the Christian doctoral students in Hebrew Scriptures who jockeyed for locking desk space in the surprisingly cozy room, I was quite content to store my books in a carrel in the basement down in the regular Divinity School stacks, where most of the other first year students were similarly assigned.

Usually, you could find me in one of those big, pink chairs. And so it was that shortly after class let out that memorable day, I went to look up the parable I had chosen to exegete. The passage was the parable of the sower, taken from Luke. The text reads:

> A sower went out to sow his seed; and as he sowed, some fell along the path, and was trodden under foot, and the birds of the air devoured it. And some fell on the rock; and as it grew up, it withered away, because it had no moisture. And some fell among thorns; and the thorns grew with it and choked it. And some fell into good soil and grew, and yielded a hundredfold. As he said this, he called out: He who has ears to hear, let him hear.

Piece of cake, I thought to myself. After working with the I Ching all my adult life, overflowing as the ancient Chinese text is with images of seeds, birds, rocks, and the like, surely I could find metaphysical meaning in this passage that I could use to enrich my own life and teaching. It reminded me, in fact, of one of my favorite passages from the Chinese text. In that passage, the reader is told the difference between the swamp plant and the oak as a metaphor for explaining the real question that is on many of our minds. Not why do bad things happen to good people, but why do good things happen to bad ones? The I Ching explains that good people are like the acorn, quietly putting down their roots and going about the business of growing their character and spirit. In the meanwhile, the inferior person is like a swamp plant, exploiting situations, taking shortcuts around integrity and the like, to grow huge overnight. At the time, it looks as if the evil people are the successful ones, waving their fronds about arrogantly in the sun while the tiny acorn's little green shoot may have not even yet broken through the dirt. But take a look the next morning. The swamp plant will have been long gone, while the acorn is on its way to becoming a mighty oak.

I could take comfort from a passage like this. Certainly, as I'd advanced my career as a writer at an acornlike pace over the past ten years, I'd seen a number of newcomers in the field of spirituality and business—more than a few of them old-style success motivational wolves in spiritual sheepsuits—sweep the media away in a frenzy of notoriety, then quietly fade away from the scene as fast as they came. The fact that even three thousand years ago, other souls in other circumstances had needed to find a way to come to grips with similar emotions helped undercut my arrogant tendency to feel singled out by fate for special attention. Beyond that, I thought the advice was good— even if in my life, there were more than a few swamp plants that hadn't yet gotten the message that they'd already had their day in the sun.

And so I went to work on the parable of the sower, using the I Ching as my inspiration. While the class had been instructed to begin by researching the history and thoughts of previous scholarship, I felt sure that what I would find would support my soon-to-be-authorized fresh, creative, but well-grounded reading of the text. By the time I was through with it, I would have exegeted the real meaning, my results not only earning me Buttrick's praise but also helping Christians as well as Jews understand better what Jesus was really trying to say. Of course, the sower was God and the seeds were God's wisdom. For the seeds to sprout, they had to fall on receptive ground. The receptive ground was anyone who would take the time to pay earnest attention to God. Everyone else was birds, thorns, and rocks—the parable's equivalent of the swamp plant. Humming, I carried my handiwork over to the volumes to complete the assignment, albeit in reverse order, checking my results against the tradition of scholarship these books contained. Our interpretation could and hopefully would reflect original thinking, Buttrick had told the class. But at the same time, it needed to be in conversation with the tradition. Otherwise, what was to stop people from allegorizing everything in the text?—just the way a number of Christians over the centuries had hijacked the various symbols and characters of the Hebrew Scriptures to satisfy strictly self-serving Christian purposes.

For example, because the Hebrew Scriptures insist that the prophet Elijah would return to earth to announce the arrival of the Messiah, some Christians teach that John the Baptist must have actually been the prophet Elijah. The teaching continues, despite the fact that within the pages of the New Testament, itself, John the Baptist denies this explicitly. Another example is the reading into every use of the word "lamb" in the Hebrew Scriptures a reference to Jesus. Sometimes a lamb is just a lamb.

Beyond such direct hijackings, there is an unfortunate school of Christian exegetes who routinely take portions of the Hebrew Scriptures out of context to support whatever their particular point of view happens to be. Unhappily, the later apocalyptic books of the Hebrew Scriptures, with their theatrically poetic imagery of death, doom, and destruction at the end of time, lend themselves to fear-mongering. For example, taking advantage of the Hebrew prophets' colorful language, contemporary fundamentalists read current events back into ancient text as confirmation that the cataclysmic intervention in the world promised by God in biblical times will occur in the near future. Fundamentalists base their predictions on passages in the Hebrew Bible's books of Daniel and Ezekiel (along with the New Testament's Book of Revelation, and later chapters from Mark and Matthew). Describing forces rather than historical events, the symbolic visions and nightmares in the original texts have been ascribed creatively by modern-day interpreters as referring to particular contemporary persons, nations, and institutions. The United Nations, the pope, environmentalists, Democrats, AIDS, and of course, today's Jews, all play prominent roles in their interpretations of apocalyptic scenarios. But while liberally citing biblical texts, often out of context, to paint their dark-hued portraits of current and future times, many of the interpretations that are accepted by the majority of millennial fundamentalists find their origins not in the Bible but in the opinions of John Nelson Darby, a nineteenth-century cleric, whose interpretations of the end of times, issued in 1909, contradict the previously established mainstream Christian tradition. Darby claimed that he was privy to personal revelation that gave the true contemporary meanings of the symbolism to him alone. Today, tune into any satellite cable religious channel and you will hear Darby's opinions as if they were issued by Jesus Christ, himself.

Just as there are many today who believe that the year 2000 is ordained by biblical prophecy to denote the end of the world as we know it, so there have been many in the past who were equally sure that the world was going to end in their lifetime.

- In the New Testament, Mark said that his present generation would not pass away before the Kingdom of God was established on earth and Christ would return.
- Joachim of Floris predicted that the millennium would begin in 1260.
- Many Christians believed that the French Revolution initiated the countdown to the end of the world, set to take place in 1800.
- William Miller, founder of the Seventh-Day Adventists, set the end of the world for 1843.

We are still here. We are still waiting. The question that needs to be considered by both Christians and Jews is not whether the world is going to end in our lifetime but rather, how are we to behave? What moral and ethical principles shall we follow, regardless of when and whether the Messiah comes to redeem us?

Unfortunately, fundamentalists who concentrate on their fanciful interpretations of the apocalyptic texts, taking particular passages of Hebrew Scripture out of their larger contexts, can easily defy the greater meaning of our holy writings to place a self-serving emphasis on personal salvation rather than on the self-sacrifice that is the ethical core, the heart and soul of scripture's message. They defy the Hebrew Scripture's reverence for creation when they allow their certainty of the end of the world to turn their focus away from environmental concerns. Why sacrifice our present conveniences just to save a rare species of bird, if the world is going to end soon any way? Because of their misuse of scripture, some fear any efforts to unite the Mideast in peace. Others develop an unhealthy acceptance, bordering on impatient anticipation, of the threat of nuclear war: a sign that

Armageddon is upon us, hastening the time when there will be a new heaven and earth.

In addition to taking text out of context and ascribing concrete meaning to symbolically poetic images, many Christians—even liberal and open-minded ones—have the tendency to string various texts together as if there were a logic in the material that does not appear in the scripture itself. Our Sunday school memory of the story of creation, Adam and Eve, is an example of this. And rarely will you hear paradoxical thoughts expressed in the same sermon: Is God vengeful and full of wrath? Or is God infused with universal love and forgiveness? We may think of Jesus Christ as the Prince of Peace, but it is Jesus himself who proclaimed: "Think not that I came to send peace on earth: I came not to send peace, but a sword" (Matthew 10:34).

The appropriation of one tradition by another is not limited to Christians. Some New Age writers do the same with Native American texts and traditions, for example. Plenty of fallen-away Jews and Christians have gone through at least a passing phase calling themselves "Running Dog" or "Butterfly Heart," lighting sage and beating a drum to the dismay of the Native Americans themselves. What constitutes honoring, learning, and sharing another's tradition—and what is exploiting and demeaning it? My classmates and I passed around a newspaper article reporting a press conference held by a Pygmy group. They accused a cult of hippy pseudo-Pygmies of completing the pillaging of their heritage (which cattle ranchers had begun a century ago) by offering superficially understood, and sometimes totally fictional, mystical, and spiritual Pygmy practices for sale in the form of best-selling books and workshops. As I began my divinity school career, issues related to the exploitation and misappropriation of other cultures was a hot topic, much on everybody's minds.

Surely I could find a way to bring my own intelligence and spirit to the parable of the sower without betraying the Christian understanding of the text. But as I opened one of the exegetical encyclopedias to read the mainstream history of Christian interpretations, certain words and phrases leaped off the page and burned my eyes. I had the general sense of the parable down, all right. But sometimes the details can make a heck of a lot of difference. The sower, the New Testament experts agreed, was not God but Jesus. And the hard ground and thorns and rock upon which the seeds fell to their death? They were not just those who wouldn't listen—but those who could not. Those very same individuals who in other nasty passages scattered throughout the New Testament were deaf to Jesus' message. And guess who these obtuse, willfully deaf people were? *The Jews.* I turned to another book hoping that the experts I had consulted might be exceptions rather than the norm. The next book was worse. The thorns, I read, refer to the crown of thorns Jesus was forced to wear by the Jews to his crucifixion: a mockery of his Kingdom of God. This parable, in fact, directly alluded to the accusation that it was the Jews who killed Christ—the linchpin of thousands of years of anti-Semitism.

Somehow my universally applicable interpretation of the parable of the sower suddenly appeared to me to be incredibly naive. I was almost defeated, but not quite. For Buttrick had said we had to be in conversation with the Christian tradition: he did not say every and all aspects of Christianity. I had one trick left up my sleeve. In San Francisco, I had befriended a prominent minister of a metaphysical church. The church had invited me to present my thoughts on spirituality and business on several occasions, to great response. At the conclusion of my most recent workshop, the minister had presented me with a copy of the *Metaphysical Bible Dictionary*. Because I knew of the church's emphasis on a loving, inclusive God and the replacement of Jesus Christ the Messiah with Christ Consciousness—a spiritual experience akin somewhat to the Jewish concept of Shekinah, the Indian concept of Krishna, the Chinese concept of Tao, and so on—I thought surely, here, I would find the Christian tradition with which I would resonate. I turned to the appropriate section and began to read: "The Jews were always the hardest to reach with the new thought. They were very set in their religion, and they usually refused even to listen to new teachings of Truth . . ."

I slammed the book shut and stormed out of the library heading toward the one person at the Divinity School who I thought might possibly be able to help me with my problem: Professor A.-J. Levine.

# 6

# Professor Levine's Office Hour

Since Professor Levine had come to take on a full professorship at Vanderbilt three weeks earlier, I'd heard from various students that she was intimidatingly brilliant, incredibly compassionate, intolerant of sloppy scholarship, and the most energetic person they'd ever met. The few doctoral students who were taking both Buttrick's and Levine's courses regaled us with stories about how she walked into the classroom on the first day of school dressed in a snappy bright red-and-black cinch-waisted suit and impossibly high spiked heels, which she immediately kicked off, proceeding to lecture at breakneck speed, virtually dancing around the room in bare feet. But it wasn't just her sense of theater that the students spent hours and hours talking about after class. It was the knowledge she was imparting to them. She knew the New Testament. To hear about A.-J., one might well wonder how a woman of under forty years had accumulated so much knowledge. But to know A.-J. was to understand that she lived her life double-time, with no signs of slowing down.

Outside the walls of the Divinity School, the response in Christian circles, who by and large had not yet had the chance to meet A.-J., ranged from curiosity to nervousness to outright hostility that a Jew had been given the prestigious professorship in New Testament scholarship, an unusual and courageous choice by the Divinity School leadership. Jewish circles buzzed, too. What was her agenda, after all, a Jew devoting her life to studying the one book most of her people would never dare even consider opening up? As people both inside and outside the community began making contact with our new professor, reports started coming back that were ninety percent awe and ten percent terror. I'd heard enough to know that if I were my normal self—the author of six books published by major New York houses, someone who had founded and co-owned one of the country's top public relations agencies for twenty-five years—she was the kind of woman I would try to befriend. But as a first year student, intimidated even by doctoral students little older than my son, I was anything but my normal self.

The ratios of awe and fear were reversed as I approached her office. I'd already heard that she was almost always there working and that her door was always open to the students. But I wasn't just *the students*—I was the Jewish student. I would know things, feel things, be vulnerable to this professor in a way the Christian students would not. If she were really a messianic Jew, for instance, a Christian in Jewish guise who believed that Jesus was the Jewish messiah, I would sniff that out in a minute. I would feel it my duty as one of the few Jews in the school to unveil her charade and bring her down. Or I would discover that the welcome to the school I'd felt as a Jew had really been an elaborate charade to reel me in to the Gospel's Good News. Nashville had its share of messianic Jews, Christians who wore yarmulkes and followed many of the traditional Jewish practices and holidays, but often with their own special twists. For example, on Passover, the seder wine in Elijah's cup was symbolic of Christ's blood: How Jewish is that?

Or at the other extreme, was she a devout, practicing Jew who would sniff down her nose at my eclectic spirituality? Would I be judged by her to be less of a person because I'd left the fold? That was, in truth, my bigger concern.

Until Jered's charge, I hadn't felt the particular need to seek out the other Jews in the Divinity School community, although I was acutely aware that they were there. The one time I did reach out was a terrible disappointment. Marvin, one of Barr's inner circle of graduate philologists, had one of the more visible and desirable student jobs, working check-out at the Div library. At that post, the student workers were privy to all the best gossip in the school and could usually be counted on to know which professors gave the hardest tests, which students were dating, which denominations were hiring, and the like. While Marvin was obviously well-liked around the school, respected both for his impeccable scholarship and the great beer parties he threw at his off-campus apartment, our relationship got off on the wrong foot after he found out that I was at the Div School pursuing my Masters of Theological Studies. In the academic lexicon, the M.T.S. was generally considered to be more of a professional than an academic degree. That means that its primary purpose is to prepare students for work in religious or social services or to provide people in related fields, doctors and lawyers (and at least one writer), with an adjunct degree supplementing their primary professional focus. In other words, the M.T.S. was a way of giving individuals who did not want to become ministers access to formal religious and theological training. Because the M.T.S. generally did not lead to the kind of academic fellowship studies post at Harvard that Marvin was heading for, the M.T.S. students were at the bottom of the Div School hierarchy—behind the ministerial Masters of Divinity students, the straight-ahead academic Masters of Religion students, and of course the doctoral elite.

"Why are you doing that?" he asked.

"It's a way for me to expand my spiritual horizons, to learn more about what those who came before me have thought about God. That's why I'm attracted to theology."

"Theology? Jews don't do theology. Theology is a Christian term."

"Jews don't think about God in a disciplined way?" That's what I thought theology meant: the disciplined effort to think about God. Theology as I had been introduced to it through the school interviewing process embraced the search for enhanced meaning and understanding that finds its roots in the study of our ancient and traditional texts, advancing the dialogue in conversation with contemporary issues. "Don't Jews do that?"

"Well, I'm sure as heck not here to do that," Marvin responded.

"Then why are you here?"

"I don't believe in God. I believe in grammar. Hebrew grammar. Grammar can teach us about the past: how ideas are transmitted through language, to evolve and change over time. It's a scientific study. But to look for meaning? And understanding? In the Hebrew

Scriptures? Forget it. How do you explain that in one text, God is loving and in another, God is pissed off? Sometimes God rewards and punishes. Sometimes God loves us unconditionally. How do you make any sense of that? It's all about projection. You can find anything you want in there. Only those with enough chutzpah to pick and choose according to their preferences and prejudices get anything at all out of the book. And then, since they are doing the picking and choosing, whose Truth is really being discerned? God's—or theirs? My assessment of Hebrew Scriptures is that for people who had previously been killing their firstborns and having sex in the fields to ensure a good crop, it was an obvious improvement. But relevant today? Forget it."

"And yet, you consider yourself a Jew. Why?"

"Great matzoh balls!"

After that exchange, I had intended to go it alone. I did not feel that I needed ongoing interaction with the Jews in this community in order to to get from the Hebrew Scriptures and my religious studies as a whole what I had come to Div School for. That, I said to myself, was strictly a matter between God and me.

But somehow things had now changed. Perhaps it was worth the risk to reach out and see whether, even if Marvin's and my relationship had not gotten very far, there might be some comfort in connecting to at least one Jewish colleague in the school. An advocate, a teacher, a friend. Was such an extraordinary outcome possible? Quietly I asked: "Professor Levine? Do you have a minute?"

Professor A.-J. Levine's office was a hurricane of papers. Her walls were lined with books of both Christian and Jewish scholarship. Her floor, part of her elaborate filing system, was covered with at least a dozen books and articles in progress strewn in this corner and that. Students' papers in varying stages of being extensively critiqued were strewn across both the unoccupied chairs.

"Sure. Clear a spot and tell me what's on your mind."

My mind? Images of Christ's blood in the Passover Cup, Sarah in the Pharaoh's brothel, Rabbi Bear banishing me from his office, Jered's angry red face: What was on my mind?

I started to tell her about what had happened in Barr's class, but she interrupted me. She'd heard about that. And that I'd already been told about the Marcionite heresy. She'd been looking forward to my visit.

Scary.

"So what can I do for you?" she asked.

Suddenly I was less interested in talking about Jered than I was in finding out about her.

"Professor Levine, can you explain to me why a Jewish woman is teaching New Testament at a Christian Divinity School?"

"Of course, if that's what you really want to talk about."

A.-J. leaned forward, telling me about her odyssey, beginning with life in a little village in the New England of the 1960s, where her father owned a fleet of scallop boats in a largely Catholic community. Among the everyday childhood taunts all children endure, A.-J. had been faced with a peculiarly specific accusation. "You killed our Lord," a schoolmate had told her matter of factly.

"How could I have killed Christ? I didn't even know the man." A.-J. laughed, somehow having turned her most unpleasant memories into inspired scholarship and a life of deep meaning. Incongruously, I noticed that she had, as was her reported habit, kicked off her shoes.

"When I asked the kids what they were talking about, they said it was written in the Bible. So somehow I got hold of a New Testament and started to read. I wanted to understand what they were talking about. What did their book say the Jews had done, and what was the truth? As my education continued, I discovered the field of biblical scholarship: academic thinkers at major universities around the world who over the past fifty years had made remarkable progress in sorting through the original texts and subsequent interpretations to distinguish literary images and ideological agendas from historical fact and probability. What was the real content of Jesus' ministry? What were the true circumstances of his crucifixion? What were the political, social, and religious problems facing the earliest churches that would have resulted in the unhappy accusations of my, and many, Jewish childhoods? Once I started reading, I never stopped. Now I know a lot. And thankfully there are churches and universities that, despite what at first glance might appear to be a challenge to their faith, want to know too."

Now it was my turn, but I did not get very far. For she didn't particularly want or need to hear about my career as a writer, my track-record of successes. What she really wanted to know was this:

"Why were you so surprised by Jered's comment?"

Why? I took a mental inventory of my life as a Jew. I had gone to grade school in a predominantly Jewish suburb of Chicago. Nobody had ever accused me of killing Christ. In fact, my earliest impression of Christians was that they had to go to school on Rosh Hashanah while the rest of us got the day off to dip apples into honey at the children's service, then off to family tables laden with rich textures, tastes, and smells. I felt sorry for them. By the time my Jewish stream had fed into the waspy ocean of New Trier Township High School in Winnetka, Illinois, I had become used to thinking of Jews, despite our smaller numbers, as the mainstream. It's not that I didn't notice that Jews and Christians tended to leadership in different school organizations—gentiles to student senate offices and pep club, Jews to the student newspaper and yearbook, for example. Or that Christians had an extra social life beyond school dances at something called "Young Life." It's just that I thought it so happened that personally I wanted to become an editor of the school newspaper and not president of the student senate.

To all appearances, that was as far as the differences went. Gentiles and Jews wore the same madras skirts. Our hair was cut in the standard style of the mid-60s, long, straight, and limp. We wore circle pins on our starched Peter Pan collar blouses and stuck pennies in our shiny loafers. I had heard that some of my classmates lived in Kenilworth, a town that had only within the last decade lifted its ban on selling homes to blacks and Jews. And while I was secretly repelled whenever anyone gave me a Kenilworth address, I did not think that their prejudices applied to anyone like me. Neither did it ever occur to me that there was anything theological underpinning the crosscurrents that prescribed the formulated pattern of our social lives.

By the time I graduated from high school, all I knew was that I was hungry for a bigger world. I dreamed of going to Berkeley where people just like me were adventuring beyond the scripted proprieties of their childhoods into a new age of expanded religious and intellectual freedom and exploded boundaries. I finished my prolonged response to A.-J.'s question by sharing with her my story about Rabbi Bear and my subsequent exile from all institutions Jewish. Until Jered's comment, I had, at best, a *Fiddler on the Roof* feeling of sentimentality about certain aspects of my tradition—most of them related to food. At worst, I felt that the temple I grew up in had been sterile and detached. But even as I explained all this to Professor Levine, I felt that somehow the whole Jered incident was turning around on me. For some reason, then beyond my grasp, I had slipped into a defensive mode, shifting uncomfortably in the wooden chair in A.-J.'s office. Her next question only made matters worse.

"So, you feel alienated from Judaism. You say that despite your avid interest in spiritual matters, the Jewish world cast you aside. The rabbis, the writers, the scholars—they abandoned you. But let me ask you a question. In all these years, did you ever once proactively engage them? Did they perhaps sense that their response to your complaints would go unheeded? Did they even know that you considered yourself Jewish? What was your part in this?"

My part? The thought had never occurred to me. I had been cast out by my tradition. That I had played any role in this other than victim had never once crossed my mind. Her mere suggestion of this sent me into an inner fury. And at that moment the object of my anger did not seem to be either Jered or myself, but Professor A.-J. Levine.

If A.-J. knew, she held her feelings close to her chest. I realize now that she was used to sitting in her office faced with angry students, blaming her for the loss of their favorite childhood stories. Over the years, I came to understand that there was great care taken in these confrontations and that she was sure I would come through. But I did not know it then.

She sat quietly for a long second, and then with a stern sort of smile, let me know that we were for the moment through. She invited me to come back again to talk. *Fat chance,* was what crossed my mind. As I was about to leave the room, she called out lightly after me: "So, where are you going for New Year services?"

# 7

## Jewish New Year

As the Jewish High Holy Days rapidly approached, the inquiries about Judaism from my Div School friends picked up pace. Carlton, who wanted to prepare himself for the serious responsibility of serving the needs of Jewish soldiers should he ever find himself on a faraway battlefront on Rosh Hashanah or Yom Kippur, wanted to know where one purchases a sheep horn shofar. Could he personally learn how to sound in the New Year by blowing on it? Did I know someone who could give him lessons?

Willow came up to me after class and asked if she could come with me to services. How should she dress? Did she need to wear a hat?

Was this a conspiracy pressuring me to go?

I had, in fact, been dully turning over the thought that maybe this year I would actually go to temple for services—even before A.-J.'s rude interview, which, when I thought about it, still made me ache with anger. Having passed the full cycle of a year in Nashville, this would be our first real High Holy Days in Nashville—the first to count, anyway. I needed to come up with some kind of strategy, some way to deal with the High Holy Days in this new, foreign land.

Back in Mill Valley, California, we'd had the ideal set-up. An ad hoc New Age Jewish congregation that emerged from the ethers like Brigadoon, a couple of times a year for the key Jewish holidays. The temple, Shabbos Shul, was led by two charismatic rabbis, brothers who blithely mixed the Orthodox trappings like tefillin and robes of their upbringing with Eastern meditation techniques, Indian chanting, and a combination of Jewish and Sufi dancing of our generation and geography. Like many who were attracted to their heart-filled praise and adoration, our ephemeral community sated my desire to be part of something larger than my individual family unit without making any more demands upon us than that we pay for our ticket at the door. Even though I'd seen many of the hundreds who gathered three times a year for ten years, I only knew three or four of them by name. And those I knew primarily from outside business networks, not in conjunction with anything specifically Jewish. Had we not made the move to Nashville, my family and I would have easily and happily been attending High Holy Day services in Shabbos Shul's rented community center gymnasium that first year. But instead, so newly arrived from our home in Mill Valley, California, that we still had not fully unpacked, I could find nothing even remotely akin to Shabbos Shul. In fact, I had only uncovered the traditional Jewish options: Reform, Conservative, or Orthodox

Suspecting that we would not fit in anywhere that first Rosh Hashanah, so soon after our arrival in Nashville, I had nevertheless kept the kids home from school and Dan and I had taken them for a walk at the wildlife preserve near our new home, known as Radnor Lake. Under the trees, we each wrote our private hopes and dreams for the New Year in special journals I had purchased for us. We returned ten days later on Yom Kippur to make lists of varying lengths of those things we had done for which we hoped to make amends. Somewhere along the way I'd heard about an old Jewish tradition that I thought we should try. Each of us tore a page from our journal, privately placing upon it our largest transgression for which we hoped to be forgiven. Rumpling the pages up, we threw them into the freshwater creek that ran rapidly off the placid lake and deep into the mysterious reaches of the fertile, green woods, watching as they bumped their way beyond our sight. Our family felt drawn together by these simple rituals. In the closeness, I felt God's presence embracing us. I knew that God was with us, even through all the ups and downs of my spiritual wanderings. God, I felt, was less concerned about how and when I chose to worship and more willing to respond to the deepest yearnings of my heart, however they happened to manifest in my life.

But at the same time, I was painfully aware of the difference between spending the High Holy Days as four people alone in a new place and sitting among hundreds of other Jews in a designated house of worship, even if it was a rented community center gymnasium. Did I, as A.-J. suggested, bear responsibility for my disenfranchisement from traditional Judaism? There was only one way to find out. I did not want to impose my own unreconciled memories of institutional Judaism on my family. But had I gotten it wrong? Perhaps things had changed. So this time around, I decided that after our family performed our simple ritual, I would foray out alone into the foreign turf of Nashville's synagogues. If Willow wanted to come with me, all the better. That would make it kind of a Divinity School assignment: an ecumenical field trip out of which perhaps we could each get a school paper. In fact, Buttrick was more than happy for me to bring a critical eye to the services, generously calling forth from the richness of his computer's bibliographical database a list of resources from the school's Jewish library that would get me started.

But there was more in it for me. I knew the presence of God in my life. I knew God in my forest walks and in my ashram meditations; I knew God on mountaintops, and I knew God in the stories of Indian mystics. God was just about everywhere in my life, everywhere, that is, but in a traditional Jewish temple. Could I find God in a Jewish temple this New Year's? I made a strategic plan. I would hit the Orthodox synagogue first. I had, after all, grown up in Reform Judaism and I thought I already knew what that was all about: intellectual Jews who had rationalized the lifeblood out of the tradition, along with all the richness of ritual life. Maybe it was Orthodoxy that contained the spiritual secrets of my faith. If I had placed sacred shawls on my shoulders and chanted Sanskrit in incense-filled ashrams, I could do this. And perhaps here, in what I thought might be the more serious expression of true Judaism, I would find the religion's soul.

Willow could not make the Orthodox morning service, but begged me to return to temple for a second time in the afternoon. She had heard about a new Reform congregation that had just come together in the rented space of a former disco. This, too, sounded promising, reminiscent of the happy times I'd spent in the rented community center with the rabbi brothers. All right, it would be the Orthodox Sherith Israel for me alone in the morning and the Reform Congregation Micah with Willow in the afternoon. If God were there, I told myself, I would know it.

It's one thing to read about Orthodox services. It's another thing to experience them for yourself. I had only been in an Orthodox temple twice before in my life, the first time when I was very young. My father had taken me to worship at his family's shul in Chicago, crowded with immigrants who had imported the rituals of the rural Russian shtetl as best they could into the crowded urban setting. In the great wave of immigration that transplanted the residents of entire villages to cities like New York and Chicago in the decades before and after the turn of the century, multiple village-based shuls sat, often side by side, offering an oasis of familiarity in the heart of their urban ghettos. Because I was so young, they'd allowed me—a female—to remain with my father on the main floor. Maybe they hadn't realized I was a girl. I was not aware of any other women present, but I now realize that they had been seated in balconies behind screens high above the floor. I remember standing among the men, who were covered with enormous shawls. Many of them were completely enveloped under their self-made bright white tents, bobbing back and forth in the early morning light streaming in through the shul's yellowed windows. Even while the majority of them prayed, a substantial minority wandered in and out and about the room, chattering among themselves. This singular memory is rich with human emotion: the warmth, the intensity, the community, the noise, the chaos that captures the essence of the Jewish worship of my grandfather's generation. For them, decorum was not even a consideration, any more than it would be in the privacy of their own homes and families. For this is what shul was for them: the living room of their Father's home, an intimate, informal place where they could talk personally to God. In the cacophony of Hebrew, Yiddish, and broken English, the voices in shul boldly lodged their complaints, sang their praises, and engaged their neighbors in conversation knowing, all the while, that all this transpired in the presence of God.

For those many of us in the 1950s whose parents subsequently migrated to the suburbs to build modern temples with regimented pews, leaving behind the embarrassing emotional excesses and chaotic worship of the shtetl, the sheer physicality of the spontaneous worship of our grandparents' generation is as foreign to us as the villages from which they came. But the emotional component in the Jewish tradition traces it roots as far back as the ecstatic swoons of a King

David and the heartfelt entreaties by prophets and patriarchs addressed both to God and to Israel. I read in one of the books Professor Buttrick had pointed me toward that the spontaneous tradition of emotion-filled prayer, juxtaposed to formal liturgy, is legitimized by its Hebrew name *Kavvanah*. I, too, wanted to feel the ecstatic swoons of a King David, the prophetic sense of hearing my name called by God—and I wanted to feel it in a traditional Jewish context. And so it was that I prepared myself to set aside my modern sensibilities and dip my toe into old, old memories that were never truly fully mine.

It was easy to find the Orthodox shul, Sherith Israel. Every synagogue in Nashville had traditionally been located on the very same street, West End Avenue, the major thoroughfare that ran through the west side of town. As if dictated by some higher commandment that proclaimed "Honor thy Street Sign," the synagogues ordered themselves along the road, with Sherith Israel at the head of the line. Next came the Conservative congregation, then the Reform congregation. As West End Avenue undergoes a name change into Highway Seventy, one finds the Jewish Community Center that used to be the end of the line: bookend to Sherith Israel circumscribing the geography of Jewish life in Nashville. But the year before, the newest Reform temple, Congregation Micah, had moved into its temporary quarters, the former discotheque, breaking tradition by moving a block off the thoroughfare, to much wringing of hands. Today I was to start my adventures at the beginning.

I had passed by Sherith Israel many times before, a nonthreatening building that fit well into the neighborhood of nursing homes, condominiums, and churches. But as I stood in the lobby of Sherith Israel, a silent stranger witnessing the husbands and wives affectionately pecking each other on the cheeks as they headed for separate entrances, I froze. I could not help thinking about the second time I'd been in an Orthodox shul. It had been a very different experience from my earlier memory. Five years ago or so, in the midst of one of my multicity book tours, I suddenly realized that when I'd agreed to these dates, I'd overlooked the fact that Rosh Hashanah was right in the middle of my tour. I was going to be in some fancy hotel in a distant city, far from family and friends. Even if I had often skipped services when I was at home, something about being so far away and alone made me frantic to find a temple. The concierge knew of a Jewish house of worship within walking distance, and so—not knowing what branch it would be or whether I would be welcome—I set out for it. It turned out to be an Orthodox shul, an urban retreat in a pleasant downtown building. As I entered the front door, I was welcomed enthusiastically and ushered toward the women's balcony. I knew that Orthodox women were seated separately on the sidelines of the sanctuary overlooking the men and boys on the main floor. Intellectually, I understood the concept of separating the men and the women so as not to mix sexual social purposes with spiritual ones. I had sat separated from the men in Swami Muktananda's ashram on many occasions and it had not bothered me. Perhaps because at the ashram, the men had simply taken the right side of the floor while we had taken the left. There was, at least to my elementary understanding, a fairness to the separation that applied to each sex equally. I was aware of the explanation that in Orthodox Judaism, women are so important and special that this relegation is really a sign of deepest respect—protecting women from the demands of public duties so that they would have their vital energies freed to reign in their own spiritual domain. Even if I had my philosophical doubts about the theory, perhaps the cadences of long passages of Hebrew—the hypnotic davening—would transport me into the sense of unity with God just as the chanting in Sanskrit had in the ashram so many times since my days at Berkeley.

And so it was that I swallowed my modern feminist sensibilities and followed one of the wives inside. She walked down the balcony aisle purposefully, quickly locating her friends. Where should I sit? There were name plaques on the benches, but was this simply an honor—or a reservation? I made my way timidly down the aisle, finding an empty seat next to the banister. Happily, there was no screen obscuring our vision and so I could fully take in the scene displayed before me. It was as if I were watching a movie of my favorite Jewish childhood memory, but from a distance above and apart. There again were the men in their shawls, the davening, the casual conversation. The rabbi, fully bearded, chanted the Hebrew, sometimes alone, sometimes joined by several or all of the men. But this time, I was not on the floor among them, immersed in the divine conversation, the hypnotic weaving of bodies draped in white. This time, I was in the balcony, straining to capture the essence of what was going on over the loud voices of the two women in the bench behind me who were enthusiastically sharing the details of somebody or other's operation.

Where were we in the service? I flipped through the pages of the prayer book, glancing around the balcony to take my cue from somebody's open page. Only one among us, a young woman in her twenties in the most forward seat of the balcony, even had her book in hand. She avidly recited the prayers, a lonely figure too far away for me to conveniently copy. The pages were all in Hebrew anyway, a language I had never learned, since in the day and community within which I was raised Bar Mitzvahs were meant to be for boys not girls. My brother and father knew Hebrew. My mother and I did not. So all right. I learned to fake Sanskrit. I could fake this too. In my spiritual eclecticism, I had learned that the Orthodox believe that the Hebrew language, having been the original vehicle of divine communication to humanity, contains the essence of God. Even if one does not catch the meaning of the words on a rational level, the very sounds of the language nevertheless embrace the hearer in relationship to the divine. I leaned over the balcony as far as I could go, hoping that the cadences of God's tongue would capture me. *"Twenty stitches! Can you imagine! No, not stitches, staples. Staples!"* was all I could hear. Would it be impolite to reel around and shush them—as every fiber in my being cried out to do? Even while knowing that I was a guest in their house of worship, I was about to do just that when I felt the warmth of a large bosom pressing against my side. As far as I was leaning over the balcony, one of my heftier neighbors had felt the need to lean over even farther. That I was in the way seemed no more to her than an extra layer of cushioning on the railing. Trapped beneath her body, I listened to her as she made plans with her husband to fix their nephew up with somebody's daughter. *"Can you talk to Stewart?"* Thankfully, he agreed posthaste and I was saved from further discomfort, just about the time the bearded rabbi began to speak. His sermon! Even the balcony settled down to listen. This was Rosh Hashanah, the birthday of the world. If God's presence had thus far eluded me in the balcony, at least now my mind would be led to the contemplation of God's divine delight through the rabbi's carefully chosen words.

As best as I can recall what happened next, the rabbi's sermon began by telling the congregation that he had a message for us that many of us would not like. *"If your grandchildren are not Jewish, then you are not Jewish"* was what came out next. This was the beginning of a theme that was to be worked out in excruciating detail for quite some time. Instead of the ecstatic swoons of King David, I felt myself sinking slowly into the growing cloud of guilt and shame that singled out one elderly person after another with bony fingers of accusation for the behavior of their adult children, and their adult children's adult children. The recent conversation about the operation still hung heavily in the air behind me, as one by one, I heard the women around me sigh and swallow hard. I could no longer stand it. I got up and left.

Five years later, as I stood in the lobby of Sherith Israel, I suddenly realized that reclaiming my singular childhood memory, if it were even possible within the boundaries of traditional Judaism, was not as simple as walking through the Orthodox shul's door for Rosh Hashanah services. From what I knew of Sherith Israel—the many warm and wonderful people I'd met, the inspired rabbi—I felt sure that the heart was there, and the community, and yet I belonged to another world. Faced with the only option of entry being a portal designated for women only, I knew that I could not find my way back into Judaism through the Orthodox door. I was not raised Orthodox. I was not raised kosher. I felt regret for the loss of a spiritually conscribed life, complete with its own book of rules—so much more comforting potentially than the boundless eclecticism of my own religious life. I was nostalgic for something I had never had. But even with all the regret, I did not blame my parents. I believe I have some grasp of the forces at work in their lives: stories, yearnings, history shared in bits and pieces with me over the years.

My father was the youngest of six children, the only one born in this country. My mother was one of two sisters, also the youngest. They grew up blocks apart from one another in the Jewish ghetto of Chicago's west side. Before my mother was one year old, her father died—leaving her mother, Rebecca, a widow while still in her teens, to fend for herself in her new, foreign community. In the few tintypes I have of Rebecca as a young woman, she has the tiniest waist—and the saddest eyes. There's toughness too, the set of her jaw, the rigidity of her elbow resting on a formal pedestal. Toughness she needed, raising two girls alone as an immigrant in a new country where she did not even speak the language. Rebecca worked as a cook. But her hours, schedule, and finances were such that the social worker assigned to her case did not feel that she could competently care for her daughters. The social worker took my mother, Sarah, to an orphanage where she lived for several years until Rebecca, with her tiny waist and penetrating eyes, landed a new husband, a good man and a good provider.

There were Jewish orphanages in Chicago in the early 1920s. But my mother was sent to a Christian children's home. She does not know why, only suspects that it may be because Rebecca, while fully Jewish, was considered to be a political rather than a religious Jew. She was a radical who believed that Judaism's particularities had imposed unnecessary prejudices and restrictions on her people, first in the Russian shtetl and now in the new country. The only way to get rid of religious-based restrictions on Jews was to get rid of religion, replace it with socialism, communism, any -ism that held the hope of equality—whatever the cost might be. In the old country, my grandmother Rebecca would sneak out in the middle of the night to meet with the other young people in the woods outside the village and make plans for a more perfect future. As alert ears picked out the sounds of Cossacks' horses' hooves in the distance, the young people would scatter. Rebecca's parents would take her shoes and hide them, lest the soldiers feel their soles and sense that they were warm when they should not be, proof enough for punishment. Quickly, the czar's picture was thrown up on the wall. Rebecca's family knew that if they wanted a future for themselves and their children, they would have to leave. Despite the fact that they were poor, they found a way to come to America by steerage to start a new life.

After her father died, my mother was spanked at the orphanage for wetting her bed every night. But the bigger trial came on Sunday mornings. The Christian girls would line up, pretty bows in their hair, to be taken to church. My mother would watch with the handful of other Jewish girls, left behind as the two straight lines of gentiles would leave the grounds to penetrate the mystery of God. And so it was that there came a day when my mother, seven or eight years old, quietly put a bow in her hair and joined the line. She went to church with the others, forgetting over the subsequent seventy or eighty years, all aspects of the adventure, with the notable exception of the shame and guilt that lingered on.

All my mother ever wanted to do was fit in. Like many of the young immigrants growing up in the ghettos of early twentieth century America, she wanted to be a modern American girl. The settlement houses, the Jewish community centers, the schools: a broad array of institutions sprang up to teach the upcoming generation how to speak English without an accent, how to shed babushkas for sunhats, how to get a good job and advance one's self socially and economically. My mother was a good student. She had brains, beauty, and ambition. And so it was that she attracted the attention of the youngest son of a family of six: Lloyd, the golden child, the only one in his family born in America, to whom all the older brothers and sisters would contribute to pay for his medical school. His older brothers were salesmen, dentists, and undertakers: but have no doubt, the Matzkin tree was destined to blossom forth with a doctor, my father, Lloyd.

Because my mother was poor, she was not considered to be a suitable match for Lloyd. But she was no fool. She stuck with him during his schooling. She helped him research his papers, she kept him on track as his taxed energy and ambition waxed and waned during the tenuous years of the Depression. Dad was employed by the library, drove a truck, worked for the post office, paying his way through medical school. Mom worked as a secretary, a clerk, a factory worker. And just before Dad received his M.D., to the dismay of his family, they eloped.

Despite their fears, she was a good match for my father. Sarah studied her friends, copying their social skills, their ambitions—even their names—if to her it represented progress. She liked her best friend's name, Mae, and so she took it. She saved carefully to buy a carpet for their first little apartment and then to buy a house in the suburbs. She studied the cases of exotic foods at Marshall Field's, and the American cookbooks at Kroch's and Brentano's. She made the conscious effort to drop everything she could that was considered backward or foreign. By the time I was old enough to join a temple, the only Jewish rituals that remained in our family tradition centered around Rebecca's gefilte fish, made from scratch: an all-day affair of fish heads, matzoh meal, and grinders. Gefilte fish at Passover. Potato latkes at Chanukah. Eventually the choppers and rolling pins were replaced by jars of Manischewitz from the grocery store shelf. Is it possible to return to what one has never truly known?

I stood for many moments watching husbands and wives part, each to his or her designated door. But this time I could not find the way in that was meant for me. And so it was that on Rosh Hashanah 1994, I proceeded several hours ahead of schedule to the coffee shop where I'd arranged to meet Willow, taking the time to journal in my school notebook about my yearning. And there, sipping cappuccinos, immersed in the pages of blue ink on white paper, I was able at last to have a conversation with God. I was still in exile, but, as the conversation proceeded from complaint to understanding, I felt assured that at least in terms of my relationship to the divine, I had not been abandoned.

# 8

## *Micah*

I had never before known anyone like Willow, a person who devoted every thought and expenditure of energy toward helping other people and the planet. Right after college, a small liberal arts college in the Midwest, equipped with a degree in agriculture, she'd been sent out on a church missionary effort to South America. She was the lone outsider in a tiny village, where she was dedicated to helping the native population find an alternative source of income rather than continuing to cut trees from rapidly diminishing rain forests. In the year and a half that she was there, she concentrated her missionary efforts on economics not theology. In fact, entranced by the warmth and intimacy of village life, and in particular one elderly woman whom she'd deeply befriended, she realized that these people had more to teach her about relationship to the sacred than she did them. Every morning before sunrise, she'd go out to the fields, digging irrigation trenches and planting seeds. In the heat of the afternoon, she'd sit with the women by the village well, sewing or weaving baskets. Speaking their language, they wove Willow into the fabric of their simple lives. Far away from industrialized society, Willow had felt God's presence close at hand. She had been planning to stay there forever.

Then there had been an accident. A piece of heavy equipment had fallen on her leg, crushing the bone in several places. The church sent in a helicopter and in a matter of hours she was hooked up to all the pumping and thumping machines of modern civilization in an American hospital, her time in South America unceremoniously ended. She had not even had time to say good-bye to the women at the well. When we talked, our conversation often drifted toward her plans to get back to South America. In fact, as she considered the possibility of making the switch from her Protestant denomination to her mother's Catholicism, her purposes were anything but theological. In her opinion, the Catholics simply had a better program that would enable her to get back to South America as soon as possible.

I had noticed that Willow was attracted to many of the broken birds in our class, helping Sammy with his reading when he came across one of the many texts that had not been translated into Braille, for example. When somebody did poorly on an exam or was running short of funds, you could often find Willow with them huddling in a corner of the common room offering comfort and helpful suggestions. At odd moments, I found myself wondering if in our developing friendship part of the attraction was that she also saw me as requiring some kind of repair. She never said anything about my needing Jesus Christ to complete me, but she was, after all, a Christian missionary. I just wondered.

Bringing a Christian missionary with me to Congregation Micah on Rosh Hashanah felt a bit over the edge, even for me. As we left the coffee house, I suddenly realized that even I felt something of an intruder inviting myself to High Holy Day services. What was I doing bringing Willow with me? The conversation along the way did not help matters any. Willow had asked me to explain the significance of the holidays. I remembered, as best as I could from my Sunday school days, that Rosh Hashanah was the beginning of the New Year and the anniversary of the date 5,755 years ago that the Jews believed the world was created. Rosh Hashanah, an upbeat holiday, ushers in a period of serious reflection, the Days of Awe, in which Jews are meant to review their previous year's deeds, repent their sins, and forgive those who have trespassed against them.

"Oh, so does that mean you are going to forgive Jered?"

"Jered? You think I should forgive Jered? You don't think Jered ought to be on his knees asking forgiveness from me?"

"Carol, you have to understand where he comes from. We were talking in the common room yesterday and he really feels bad about what happened. He had no idea."

"Ignorance is no excuse. Just look at all the ignorant Germans in World War II. They had no idea either."

"You are equating Jered to the Nazis?" Willow was aghast.

"There were Christians in Nazi Germany, you know. Christians who found good solid reasons within their own theology to support Hitler."

"And there were Christians who found within their own theology the directive to oppose Hitler with every means at their disposal, even if it meant sacrificing their own lives. You really should give Jered another chance."

"Then why doesn't he come to me directly?"

"Because he's afraid of you."

We rode on toward Micah in silence. Afraid of me. Could that be the real root of all evil: not money or greed, but fear? Secretly, I had my own fear. That somehow Willow's Christianity—her serene upbringing unravaged by the images of Jews burning in the fires of the Holocaust that haunted my childhood— had allowed her to grow a more generous disposition than was my own bruised and wary soul. Despite our mutual urges toward universality, I had to admit that in some deeply essential ways, Willow and I were very different. The former disco parking lot was overflowing with cars, reminding me of my quest to encounter God within the walls of my own tradition. I yearned deeply for a place to call my spiritual home. Would Micah be it? I didn't need much, I thought to myself, only that God's presence be invoked on some level, in some way, by somebody or something.

If God was at Micah that first Rosh Hashanah, I sure couldn't pick out the divine presence over the cacophony of old memories that entrance into a Reform congregation, even one as progressive and open-minded as Micah, brought up for me. Not a trace of disco remained, as I mingled with the crowds who waited to be handed a prayer book by one of the many friendly ushers on the way into the sanctuary. Behind a contemporary green stained glass window, I could see neatly aligned rows of chairs and no sign of a dance floor. There would be no line dancing here today. Nor would there be recognizable melodies to the few parts of the service I remembered. The rabbi seemed to be amiable and welcoming. In fact, he looked a lot like Rabbi Bear. While Willow got into the spirit immediately, doing the responsive readings and gamely making her way through the Hebrew transliterations, my mind kept wandering away from the pulpit and into the congregation. There were a few people in furs. A real turn-off. Somebody's baby started to cry. Unpardonable. Some people sang too loud, some not at all. Early on in the service, I decided that there wasn't enough Hebrew. As the service proceeded, I decided there was too much. And who were those special people honored by a seat on the bima? I'd heard that these former disco digs, well turned out as they were, were only temporary. Big money in the congregation had already put a down payment on a piece of land, and building on the new temple was to begin shortly. I decided it must have been the big money on the bima. As I busied myself counting the number of women wearing hound's-tooth-print jackets, that year's in look, I suddenly remembered my purpose in being there. The sermon was already in progress and I tuned in, hoping against hope that the rabbi's words would put my mind to rest and open my heart to God's presence.

The sermon, stirring as it may have been to people on the inside of Micah, sounded to me more like an annual report than the trembling in awe before the divine mystery. This was Micah's second anniversary. It had been founded by forty families, most of whom had previously belonged to the other Reform congregation, the only Reform show in town for over one hundred years. I had heard the rumors that many of Micah's founding families had walked out of that temple's congregation en masse when the rabbi, now gone, had chosen to use his High Holy Day sermon as the forum to air his belief that interfaith marriage was wrong. Based on its founding reputation for tolerance and diversity, coupled with the brilliant seduction of the well-respected and beloved Rabbi Kanter away from his Chattanooga congregation, Micah had quickly grown to four hundred families. Rabbi Kanter used this particular sermon to celebrate the miracle of this congregation's spectacular growth. While I was happy for them, as far as I was concerned there was nothing that had transpired in the hour or more since my arrival that inspired me to transcend my everyday consciousness to bask in sacred presence. Disappointed, I mumbled through the remainder of the service, preparing myself for Willow, whom I still suspected of something funny. Whether it was betrayal or sainthood, I hadn't yet decided. During the blessing over the wine at the tail end of the proceedings, I glanced over at her. Tears were streaming down her face. In fact, she was muffling quiet sobs. Then I noticed that she was clutching at her heart.

"Are you okay?" I whispered.

"More okay than I've ever been in my life," she answered.

"What do you mean?"

"I'll tell you after services . . ."

I was hurrying us toward the exit, no easy feat as people before, next to, and behind us offered us—even though we were total strangers in their midst—enthusiastic handshakes, kisses, and hugs. *"L'shana tova." "L'shana tova."* At last we were outside, in a quiet spot next to a side entrance.

"I've never showed this to anyone," Willow whispered. She reached down inside her blouse to the spot where she had been clutching her heart. Her thin fingers retrieved a long, silver object. A mezuzah!

"Where did you get that?"

"It was my mother's. She gave it to me in secret on my sixteenth birthday. I have worn it every day since."

"Your mother's? But your mother is Catholic."

"My mother was raised Catholic. But she was born Jewish. Her parents died in the Holocaust. But before they did, they hid her in a Catholic orphanage. Carol, I know that Judaism is passed down through the female line. That means I'm Jewish too."

*"L'shana tova!"* a stranger passing by hugged us both and left us standing there in stunned silence as he walked to his car and drove away.

# 9

# The Melting Pot

Because Lester was the only one in Buttrick's class who took notes on a laptop—thanks to a generous grant that he had received as an inducement to get more minority graduate students into the department of religion's doctoral program—I asked him if he would be willing to run off a copy of his notes for the class I'd missed while attending services. It was a relief, after twenty-four hours of lingering emotion, to take my mind off of Willow's confession. I put her words on the back burner to take them out to consider at some future date, when I might be better psychologically prepared.

"It was a great class," Lester reported to me over coffee in the refectory. Buttrick had charted out where we stood today in the great sweep of history. In the Middle Ages, Western culture was dominated by the church's explanation of the cosmos. God was above, man below. The meaning of life was not a question, it was a given. For all the plagues and pestilence, through the Middle Ages, the individual understood that his or her only hope for a relationship with the universe that would make sense of life was to swallow the church's point of view hook, line, and sinker.

Then came the Protestant Reformation followed by the Enlightenment, sweeping in with it the rise of scientific thought and the political uprisings of the eighteenth and nineteenth centuries, bent on clearing out all vestiges of the past in favor of the fresh air of political, economic, intellectual, and religious liberty. People like Kant had introduced the notion that human beings could use their rational capabilities to think things through for themselves. Human capability, rather than church dogma, could be counted upon to provide us with new, improved structures of meaning. In the modern era, "miracles" we once turned to as an explanation of the cosmos, were now been replicated on demand. Microscopic cameras probed the origins of life as sperms penetrate eggs on prime-time television. Skeletons are uncovered from the earth's deep stratas, filling in the gaps concerning our species' history. To many, God, as packaged and delivered by the church, seemed no more than a superstition left over from times long past. Who needed God to help us negotiate life's tragedies when the best minds in the world were working to solve whatever problems yet remained? Want to get pregnant? Don't want this or that disease? Anything we didn't learn in science classes will find its way sooner or later onto the evening news.

Religion, John Locke argued, should be based upon human reason. "Superstitious" faith practices were lower forms of religion at best. Reasoned thought would lead us to rise above the backward, separative aspects of our religions in order to join together to work toward common goals. Many of the Jews among nineteenth-century Europe's intellectual elite dismissed the emotional and mystical aspects of "primitive" folk traditions—including their own Judaism—as nonsense and fanaticism. And it wasn't only the intellectual elite. My grandmother Rebecca, after all, was a mere peasant girl living in the rural shtetls of Russia, and she shared the messianic vision of a better world to come, the cornerstone belief of Judaism, even if to achieve this goal, God must be done away with in favor of politics.

But with the rise of Hitler and the atrocities of World War II, the modern era—along with its optimistic view of human nature and the naive belief in a universal brotherhood—came crashing to an end. After a four-hundred-year run at modernism, we were in a period of cultural breakdown between epochs. Shattered and cynical, people have turned to the excesses of individualism, a consumer mentality that finds meaning in the gratification of desires for personal satisfaction rather than the prophetic call to self-sacrifice for the good of communal goals. With the exception of some millennialists, who see in our approach to the year 2000 the end of the world, the great majority of scholars who study such things believe that some new era in world history will come to take the old epoch's place. What that will be, the shape it will take, is yet to be seen. In the meantime, the best label the academic world has been able to come up with to describe our present moment is "postmodern." We do not define ourselves in academic circles today by what we are, but rather, by what we are no longer and what we are not yet.

Listening to Lester read through his notes, sprinkled liberally as they were with his own rich commentary, I put two and two together. I was born in the years just following World War II. In fact I was born in 1948, taking secret pride all my life in the fact that the modern state of Israel and I were the very same age. The suburban congregation within which I was raised was a Reform temple, a movement founded by Jewish intellectuals in the heart of the Enlightenment. It was a time in which God had been dismissed as mere superstition, the nonsense of fanatics. In the wake of the Holocaust, Jewish scholars chimed in, proclaiming "the death of God." No wonder I had to turn to Buddhist chanting and Zen meditation for spiritual nourishment.

"The universalists weren't completely wrong," I quietly suggested. "Back in California, there were a lot of us who believed that there was a mystical unity at the heart of all religion. We can move beyond our differences to become one. The problem with the old universalists is that they thought that the way to achieve this was through our rational minds. The real route is through mystical experience."

Lester took a sip from his cooling coffee, considering my unexpected response.

"Mystical experience? Of what?"

"Of divine presence."

"And how do you know when you are experiencing divine presence?"

I paused, resisting the urge to say "you just know." It was true, but I had already learned in my few weeks at divinity school that *just knowing* was the way to end a conversation quickly, and I wasn't ready to do that yet.

"It's a feeling." That was, after all, what had been lacking during my previous day's field trip to the two temples. I hadn't felt God's presence.

"Feeling, as in emotion?"

"Emotion is part of it, maybe even a big part of it. But there's something more—a certainty that is beyond words."

"You're in Barr's class, aren't you? Have you read 1 Kings 22?"

"I don't know. I guess so. I mean, I read the book of Kings. But we're moving pretty fast. Why?"

"Take out your Bible," he urged. "I'd like to hear your response."

I began to read: "And there came forth the spirit and stood before the Lord, and said: I will entice him. And the Lord said unto him: Wherewith? And he said: I will go forth, and will be a lying spirit in the mouth of all his prophets."

"What does it mean?" I asked Lester.

"In this passage, God commissions a spirit, one of God's own inner court, to lie to four hundred prophets of the Jewish King Ahab. The prophets, feeling that they have received accurate information from God, pass the lie along to their king. Now there are theological implications to this story: Does God tell lies? And there are political ones, as well: the prophets of one historical house pitted against the prophets of another. But for the purposes of this discussion, the important thing to note is that feelings are not always reliable indicators. Each one of those four hundred prophets truly felt he was prophesying God's true word. And in fact, it was God's intention to make them feel that was true. But it was all lies. Feelings aren't always reliable. If you don't want to take this message from biblical sources, certainly you are aware of the emotional manipulations of television evangelists. It's easy to play on people's emotions to make them *feel* God's presence, especially if you really believe you are in direct contact with God. In any case, I don't deny the possibility that God is at work in the universe. I even believe, as you do, that mystical forces beyond our control are urging us toward some ultimate unity, but I don't think that feeling alone is a valid indicator as to whether God is at work in one particular place or another, or not."

"Okay, Lester. I'll buy that. But if it's not feeling, then what is it?"

"You know I've got a little congregation I minister to on Sundays. Some mornings I get up, and I feel empty and alone and yet I have to preach God's word to my people. So you know what I do? I get down on my knees and I pray to God to work through me, regardless of how I'm feeling. Sometimes the spirit comes into me, sometimes even in the midst of a sermon, and I feel the congregation perking up, all ears and hearts. Other times they sit there, solid as stones. And still I believe that God is working through me and the community. God's ways are mysterious, working through us invisibly. Whether I'm feeling God's presence or not, I preach, I visit my parishioners who are bedridden, I make sure the children get fed hot breakfasts, I do what I believe God has called me to do, whether I'm feeling like it or not."

Just then Sammy walked into the refectory and hearing our voices, headed for our table, delicately balancing a big piece of cheese pizza on a paper plate.

"Hey, campers. What's buzzing? I'm in the mood for some mental jousting!" Sammy laid his cane down next to his chair and sat down without waiting to be asked. Such little intimacies, a familial sense of belonging to the Divinity School community, still gave me quiet pleasure.

"Carol is arguing for the possibility of mystical universalism as the next epoch after postmodernism," Lester cheerfully volunteered.

"I was? I thought I hadn't gotten in a word edgewise for the past half-hour!"

"Why you little rascal!" Sammy chided me. Then turning to Lester. "You never know what surprises those Berkeley hippies are going to try to pull on us next."

"I'm rather fond of the universalist model myself," Sammy offered. "We'll all ooze together in one perfect unity that will be five foot five, 125 pounds and look just like me."

"No way," Lester grinned. "We'll all sit around the campfire, singing gospel hymns. Boy. That will be sweet."

"Stop it you guys. You're making fun of me. I'm dead serious about this."

"Okay, then, " Lester said. "What's your vision?"

"I don't know. White light. Unity. Pure love. You know, transcendence."

"You mean after you die. I'll buy that," Lester replied.

"No, I mean that is the spirit that is capable of infusing how we could relate to each other in the mundanities of our everyday lives."

"Oh yes? And just how will this look, exactly?" A bit of pizza dribbled off Sammy's chin. I wondered whether it would be rude or helpful to point it out to him. Happily, he swiped his napkin at the spot and it disappeared.

"I think it will take place in stages, " I continued. "Stage one: people of all faiths and traditions will sit down at the same table, in the spirit of deepest respect possible. We will give thanks for our common humanity and the divine goodness inherent in all of God's creation."

"My God," Sammy exclaimed. "It's the story of the Pilgrims and the Indians sitting down together at Thanksgiving. You must have loved first grade!"

"Get off it, Sammy!"

"No, really," Lester offered, "Sammy's right. We were all taught that underneath the veneers of our religious, ethnic, and racial differences, we were all the same. It's the old theory of the melting pot. America offered us the opportunity to strip away our differences. But think about it for a minute. When we all get melted down together, what color, texture, and sex do you think we'll be?"

"Male, white, and Protestant," Sammy shot back.

"It doesn't have to be that way," I protested. "It could be something better than that, spiritually higher!"

"By whose standards?' Lester asked. "The Puritans thought their vision was inspired by God and therefore they were divinely empowered to impose their truth on all others."

"Fundamentalists make this attempt today, using their politics and their media," Sammy added. "I should know. My father, the minister of God, is personally trying to grow his church large enough to conquer the world."

"But even the New Age, with its mass-market approach to spirituality, picks and chooses aspects of any and all religions, melting them into a milquetoast panacea that discounts true differences as 'old mind-sets,'" Lester took over, on a roll. "Take a little from here, a bit from there. Take the parts that feel good, the parts about love and peace, and conveniently snip and paste out those aspects that are challenging, like self-sacrifice, discipleship, discernment, and the like. Every person has their own religion—God talks to each and every one directly—and the result is that they all bear a remarkable resemblance to whichever self-proclaimed self-help guru's book happens to be on the best-seller list this month. And now, as fewer and fewer people get their spirituality through organized religion, they are increasingly seeking spiritual guidance in places like the Internet. Faceless gurus transcend issues of ethnicity and race—not to mention the inconveniences of a living community—offering anonymous advice to equally anonymous seekers. So tell us, Carol. What is the true vision of unity you have for all of us?"

I looked at my watch. By golly, I had almost forgotten. That very afternoon, I was to be on a Business and Spirituality panel at the Southern Festival of Books downtown. I thought I heard Sammy snicker as I fled the refectory, but I refused to look back, lest I be turned into a pillar of salt.

# 10

# *The Festival of Books*

M y appearance at the Southern Festival of Books was my first outing as my old self, the author and speaker, since immersing myself in the altered universe of the Divinity School a little less than a month before. A lot had happened in that scant span of time—a lot had happened in just the previous hour's discussion—and I wondered if and how I could pull off my part of the panel. My task was to present the central message and point of view of my most recent business book, *How Would Confucius Ask for a Raise: One Hundred Enlightened Solutions to Tough Business Problems*. But even though it was my most recent publication, the actual writing of the book had taken place in another century, most of it while still living my previous existence in Mill Valley.

I hoped that speaking would be a lot like riding a bike: that faced with an audience of eager faces, my old persona would take over and I would dazzle them with stories culled from the ancient book of Chinese wisdom and divination. The I Ching as applied to contemporary workplace challenges. While *Confucius* had not yet won giant sales, it had picked up some very nice write-ups, including a recent rave review in the *Washington Post*. I was proud of the work that went into it and found myself relieved to discover that my belief in the contents were somehow withstanding the intellectual onslaught of the past few weeks.

The lecture room in the basement of Nashville's Legislative Plaza was packed, and I could see through the frosted window of my designated lecture hall vague elevated shadows indicating to me that my fellow panelists had already been seated. I had been so consumed by the logistics of starting school, I had not thought to find out who my fellow panelists were to be. In any case, I had done enough of these to know that I could wing it.

In fact, I didn't think anyone or anything could rattle me after ten years on the speaker's circuit. But as I opened the door and entered the room, I faced the one shadow I had not realized until that very moment I now most feared. For up at the podium, busily adjusting the shared microphone to her height, was the first panelist. Completing the task with the mike, she set her book up for display: *Thick Face, Black Heart.* It, too, was based on Chinese philosophy. But that wasn't the real problem. The problem was that she was Chinese. The I Ching was her culture, her heritage. And who was I, born and raised a Jew in Chicago, Illinois, to be writing about Confucius as if I were the expert? I felt an uncomfortable edge of competitiveness rising in me as I shook her hand, followed by the hand of the easygoing psychologist to her left, who had written a nice-enough-sounding title about humanizing the workplace.

I didn't like the set-up. After the three of us on the panel spoke for ten minutes each, there would be time for questions. At the conclusion, we would parade up to the open-air plaza on the street level above to sign books side by side. I'd been in such situations before and knew that inevitably one of us would emerge victorious. There would be a crowd of enthusiastic fans eager to get their favorite author's signature on their newly purchased books, while the others would sit quietly, autograph pen clutched hopefully in hand, trying to look busy, productive, and authorlike doing nothing.

I hoped I would be the lucky one. And I thought I had a shot at it, given the *Post* review and all. But even more importantly, after twenty-five years studying the I Ching, despite the fact that I had been raised in Jewish Chicago rather than Chinese Hong Kong, I felt that I understood the book's very soul. The ancient Chinese had great gifts of wisdom to share with us Westerners and having applied many of the principles I'd gleaned from studying the book over the years to my own business, I knew that both it, and I, had been thoroughly tested. During my ten minutes, I'd planned to cover some of the key principles in the I Ching: balance, cycles, humility, goodness, perseverance, and simplicity. I would then read a sample question from my book: Tough Business Problem #32.

*"My subordinate failed. If I act with compassion and let her know I understand, what will motivate her to try harder next time?"*

My answer:

The I Ching contends that man has received a nature that is innately good. Because this is true, it is worth taking the risk of believing that the individual in question has as much interest in rectifying and recovering from her failure—and in identifying the cause and avoiding a repetition—as you would if you found yourself in her situation. You may be making a mistake in this case—perhaps her motivation and intent are not as unsullied as you want to believe. Even so, it is better to err from time to time by placing your trust in someone who proves unworthy of your empathy than to deny forever your willingness to take a leap of faith in order to honor the compassionate spirit within yourself.

My plan would have worked out fine had I gone first rather than last. But the first panelist, Chin-Ning Chu, must have read a different version of Chinese philosphy than had I. She saw in the hidden recesses of the ancient texts—if they are in there at all—instruction for treachery and self-interest in the workplace that had escaped my years of study. She saw in the often cryptic words a roadmap to the art of deception: how to perfect the skill of misleading your adversary. "The ability to mislead an adversary has always been seen by Asians as admirable," wrote Chin-Ning in her 1991 book, *The Asian Mind Game*. "All of Creation is a game of deception." Where I saw compassion, she saw ferocity. Where I saw the middle road, she saw the relentless drive to win. Her philosopher-executives were no less than workplace warriors, brandishing their briefcases at one another like Ninjas at a Saturday matinee.

One thing I have to say for my fellow author, she truly walked her talk. Unabashedly going first, she went on in impassioned tones exhorting the audience to victory while the two of us politely waited for our turns. Finally, she relinquished the floor. The psychologist took a few of the remaining minutes and then I took mine. We opened the floor for questions.

It was apparent which of us had won the day. Every question was for the first speaker. *How do I beat out my competitor who's got a better product line than I? What do I say if I get caught in a lie?* And so on and on. Eventually a festival volunteer came and fetched us. Waddling behind her like little ducks all in a row we took our places at the signing well. Boldly lettered name plates indicated where each of us was heading. Twenty or thirty people clustered around Chin-Ning's seat. Nobody was lined up at either of our two spots. Oh well, I thought, there were worse fates than getting stuck next to a pleasant psychologist. At least I could probably get some free advice. Gamely, I took up pen in hand and waited and, lo and behold, I glimpsed three bodies out of the corner of my eye, heading purposefully my way. I turned and there were three of the happiest sights I had ever seen in my life. Dan, Grant, and Jody had decided to surprise me at the well. "Get me out of here!" was my relieved greeting to them. And we headed out for an early supper and a vivid recounting of the day's more memorable battles.

"You know, Carol," Dan said to me between bites of roasted chicken, after I pondered aloud why the audience had been so attracted to the first author's sharper-edged version of spiritual truth. "It never occurred to me to tell you this before, but I've mused on it for a long time. As I read the way you presented the wisdom of Confucius in your book, I always thought he sounded more like a Jewish rabbi than a Chinese philosopher. Maybe you should try writing a Jewish book some time."

It was nice to know that after all I'd been through I could still laugh. If I had to choose between a thousand people in line or these three loving souls, I'd choose these three over and over again. But the thought of writing a Jewish book? The notion struck me as patently absurd. "Maybe in another life," I told Dan as we turned out the lights that night to go to bed.

# 11

# *Return to A.-J.*

At the start of the next class session, Barr announced that given that there was too much material to cover in this course, he would now enforce his policy of deferring all class-time questions to the hour we spent every week with the teaching assistants. He would, however, be posting his office hours and would be happy to entertain individuals' questions and concerns one on one. After class, he came directly over to me and asked if he could please see me at my earliest convenience. He then strode briskly from the room. As the room emptied, I sat there astonished. And then, across the room, I heard Willow calling to me. She was sitting toward the back of the rapidly emptying room, huddled with Jered and waving me over. *Now what?*

"Jered's got something to say to you," Willow's soft eyes begged me to listen. The too long silence was awkward.

"Jered . . ." Willow urged him.

"Carol. What I said was wrong. I'm sorry. I had never seen a Jew before. I don't think any of my parishioners have. We just don't have any Jews in our town. The only thing we read about Jews is what's in the New Testament, and the fliers that we find on our car windows at the grocery store parking lot. Like this . . ." Jered pulled out a folded piece of paper, professionally printed with the headline: "HOPE FOR THE HOPELESS." I quickly read the boldface copy:

*The Lord's disciples knew the checkered history of the Jews well. They knew that God, on numerous occasions, had turned His back on them because of their sins and delivered them into the hands of their enemies. . . .*
*The faithful shall see those who are born in darkness, led into darkness,*

*while the righteous who have the hope of Heaven shall be exalted. The*
*hopeless sinners shall cry aloud in anguish when seeing them exalted . . .*

And so on, and on.

"Why are you showing me this crap?" I said angrily.

"Carol, I did something even worse than you know. I need your forgiveness."

This was way more than I could handle. I started to get up to leave, but Willow reached out to my arm to stop me.

"I've got two minutes, Jered. Then I've got to go."

"After class the other day, I drove home to visit with one of my parishioners who was dying in the hospital. As she lay there dying, she blamed her misfortune on the Jews and warned me to stay away from them. 'Jews?' I said to her, 'You've never even seen a Jew.' But she got this crazy look in her eye and said that they were everywhere, in secret, running everything. That under their funny hats, they had horns. And, she whispered, 'They want to drink our children's blood.' I said some prayers for her and went home shaken.

"I knew that what she was saying was untrue. In fact, having met you and Professor Levine and hearing what Barr has to say about the Hebrew Scriptures, I know that what she was saying was not only untrue, but evil. I spent the whole night in prayer, realizing that even if she were dying, I had to confront her. I was going to go straight there in the morning and beg her to rescind her sinful thoughts. But when I got there, her family was out in the hallway sobbing. She had suddenly passed and I was not able to set things right with her.

"But Willow and I have been talking. She told me about going to services with you and how wonderful Jewish people are. She said that she felt God's presence in your sanctuary, the unmistakable feeling of holiness. After all, I had never stopped to think of it before, but Jesus Christ was Jewish. She convinced me that I can still set things right with you. So I promise you, Carol, nobody will ever again in my presence, be allowed to say anything negative about Jews again, no matter what the circumstances."

The fact that I had heard Jered out was all the blessing I could offer, for this raw confrontation with anti-Semitism, even if presented in the past tense, overwhelmed my senses. I had told A.-J. Levine the other day that I had never encountered anti-Semitism in my sheltered life. Nobody had ever accused me, as they had her, of killing Christ. But this brush with evil—in fact, all the incidents of the preceding three weeks—were opening wounds in me that I did not even know I had. As I left the room, heading as bidden to Barr's office, I was not thinking of Jered's extraordinary confession however. I was thinking of what he said about Willow feeling God's presence at Micah. But of course, it would be easier for her. She did not know that she had any particular connection to Judaism until she was sixteen. For her, entry into the synagogue was some kind of romantic interlude. I wouldn't deny her the reclamation of some relationship to her heritage, but, at the same time, she was there out of choice. It would have been easy for her to spend her whole life as a Catholic or Episcopalian or whatever it was she decided. In fact, I had a suspicion that switching from one Christian brand to another was what she most probably would do. It seemed to me that this foray into Judaism was simply some kind of adventure for her, a rite of passage that would leave her enriched by her brush with Judaism, but without encountering the complex undercurrents that came naturally to someone born and raised in the Jewish tradition. Willow at age five and seven and ten and fourteen had gone to church, New Life dances, and Christmas parties, celebrating the Good News of our country's dominant religious and cultural heritage, while I was, in some deeply unexplored ways, both ashamed and terrified of that to which I had been born. There, I let the thought formulate—perhaps for the first time in my life. I was terrified of being Jewish. Who wouldn't be? Born so shortly after the conclusion of the brutal destruction of six million of my people, for no other reason than that they were what I was. Jews. When the television screens broadcasting the Eichmann trial lit up our home with horrific footage of dead bodies being bulldozed into piles, charred skulls retrieved from rusty ovens, lampshades made of Jewish flesh, I was thirteen years old.

As the young teenager sat there before the television set, the blue light of evil and destruction reflecting off her face, she had secretly made a pact with herself. They would never get her. She would be smarter, tougher, fit in better, hide better. Whatever it would take, she would find a way to be safe. And so the girl, *and so I,* had sat alone and untouched during Rosh Hashanah services. Until now I had honored my childhood pact, but the cost was great. A.-J. was right. I had not only been exiled by my people, I had also exiled myself.

As I approached Barr's office, I realized that I had forgotten to check his office hours. I knocked, with no response. And then I heard the unmistakable rapid tap, tap, tap, of high heels behind me.

"*L'shana tova!*" Professor A.-J. Levine had emerged from her office down the hall, on the way to her mail slot. "How are you?"

How was I? Drinking children's blood, horns under yarmulkes, charred skulls. Hot tears began streaming down my face. I was mortified, a grown woman standing in the university hallway face to face with someone I had hoped to impress, sobbing. A.-J. ushered me into the privacy of her office, the abundance of both her compassion and her tissue welcome, indeed.

"What did the Jews do to deserve all this?" I finally managed to gulp out between sobs. "Why did the Jews have to go kill Christ?"

"That's a semester's worth of questions right there," A.-J. said. "You're going to take 'Religion, Literature, and Faith of New Testament Times' with me next semester, right? Good. But for now, there's a couple of things you should start chewing on. For one, you keep talking about 'The Jews.' What do you mean when you say that? Remember, Jesus and his disciples considered themselves to be Jews too."

While A.-J. promised to go into more depth next semester, she proceeded to dispel my simplistic idea—the notion of many people, including an unfortunate majority of Christians—that there has ever been a cohesive, religious/social entity known as "The Jews." Out of ignorance and laziness, many people have reduced the multiplicity of Jewish sects, opinions, lifestyles, cultures, and communities that existed in the first century; along with the diversity of Jews of the Middle Ages, of the Renaissance, of the Enlightenment, of contemporary times; of Spain, of Africa, and of Russia; of Orthodox, of Reform, of Reconstructionist, of Conservative; of Israel and of Diaspora; and much, much more, into a single lump. In this way, Christians, beginning with the Gospel of John, could dismiss all Jews as being "not of God" in one fell swoop. In truth, there is ample historical evidence that the fabric of first century Judaism was as rich and diverse then as it is now. Far from the legalistic, ritualistic, spiritually dead faith that

has come down to us through Christian tradition as the Jewish lega-
cy, there is an increasing appreciation in scholarly circles, including
many prominent Christian scholars, of the deep, vibrant vitality and
spirituality in the Jewish landscape of the first century. This truer portrait does not attempt to gloss over controversies, conflict, and disagreements between different strands of Judaism then or now. In fact,
it stands proudly in the tradition of the Hebrew Scriptures. There the
freedom to question, to struggle, to disagree, and to debate—not in
defiance of God but in the earnest effort to discern and live out God's
will—is considered by many to be the central dramatic theme of the
Jewish tradition.

"Next semester we'll explore in some depth how to avoid the pit-
fall of entering the debate about who killed Jesus at the level of
whether it was really the Pharisees or the Sadducees, which group of
Jews was really the bad ones," A.-J. said. "But before you get too overwhelmed with all this, let me address the second part of your
question: Why did the Jews kill Jesus? What makes you so sure any
of these groups did? In truth, the historical probability is that they did
not. Evidence points to the probability that Romans crucified Jesus.
Crucifixion was a Roman, not a Jewish, form of punishment. And it
betrays common sense to imagine that any such politically disempow-
ered group, any non-Romans of the first century, should suddenly
start ordering the Roman official Pontius Pilate to do anything, let
alone kill Jesus."

"Then why point the finger at the Jews?"

"There were political forces in play, struggles for power between
the various religious sects and groupings that had emerged out of the
boiling pot of the first century."

I learned from Professor Levine that among those who emerged
from within Judaism to believe that Jesus really was the Jewish Messiah were some who felt threatened by those—often their very own
mothers and fathers—who felt no need to join in. As Jesus' followers
soon discovered, the vast majority of Jews felt no need for Good
News. They were already fulfilled in their relationship to God and
their tradition. They refused to buy the line that in Jesus had come the
Jewish Messiah who, in their understanding of Judaism, was meant to
usher in the messianic age: a time of everlasting love and peace on

earth. As the first generation of apostles who knew Jesus personally began dying out and the Kingdom of God on Earth had not yet arrived, the need to transmit the story of Jesus' life and death to writing became a priority. Thus the New Testament was not written by Jesus, nor was it written during his lifetime. The versions of the story that have come down to us, the versions that accuse the Jews of killing Jesus, were written thirty to sixty years after his death, in times, circumstances, and places very different than Jesus' own time. One of the biggest questions these subsequent generations of Christians had to answer, the question that the very existence of Jews who did not climb aboard the Jesus bandwagon waved in their face, was this: *If Jesus was the Messiah, where was the messianic age his arrival was supposed to bring with it?*

As Christians hurried about the Mideast, North Africa, Asia Minor, and Europe bringing their Good News to the heathens and pagans of ancient towns and villages—having more or less given up on converting the majority of the Jews of their times to their Good News—they had good cause to worry that the Jews, who believed the Messiah was yet to come, might get there first. Pagans who encountered Judaism found it an attractive religion, indeed. Even before the birth of Christianity, groups of non-Jews, known as godfearers, routinely hung around the outer courts of the synagogue. They were fascinated by the philosophy and the ritual.

True, as Christianity evolved, it added a few marketable bells and whistles: the ability to convert males without requiring them to undergo circumcision, for example. But it was apparent to many in the first centuries following the birth of Jesus that Judaism as a philosophy, as a moral structure, and as a way of life was working quite well for a whole lot of people. It wasn't until the third century, when Constantine made Christianity the state religion and banned attempts at proselytizing by all other traditions and sects, that choosing between Judaism and Christianity was no longer an option.

Various communities of the early Jewish people as proselytizers? I had heard that in our times, there were some groups of Jews— Orthodox, mostly—involved in something called Jewish outreach. But my impression was that this had mostly to do with trying to get fallen-away Jews like me to return to the fold. But imagine Rabbi

Siskin, the austere intellectual rabbi of my youth, putting flyers about the transformative power of the Sh'ma on windshields in parking lots! It was such an odd thought that from some unknown depths issued a little laugh.

"That's better," A.-J. said. "This was a good start today. You'll make it through just fine. Just don't let it get to you. Here, let me loan you some of the books we'll be working with next semester. Fredricksen is particularly good on these kinds of issues. You might want to take a look at her. And I would suggest you go to the library and take a look at the anti-Semitism literature. Of course, if any more questions come up for you this semester, hightail it in here. When I'm not in class, I'm usually here."

I left her office, the additional books weighing down my back-pack. I didn't mind the burden, for I knew that the tonnage in the black canvas sack with embroidered trim, a back-to-school-after-twenty-four-years present from Dan, was physical knowledge just waiting to become part of my mind. This was a new thought, since one of the attractions of Eastern and Indian mysticism had been the quelling of the mind. I'd written a whole book, *Solved by Sunset,* on how to empty one's mind in order to resolve the sticky issues that stubbornly manage to resist one's routine left-brain problem-solving techniques. In it my primary interest had been to counterbalance the extremes of the rationally powered will and drive, which aim to put us rather than God in the driver's seat of our lives, with the inner knowing of intuition, creativity, the divine wisdom of the uncon-scious-right brain, or whatever it is you want to call it. I never said that people should not use their rational minds. If you can solve some-thing using logic and rational thought, why not? If your problems will resolve that way, then do it. But if you've come to the end of your normal problem-solving processes and you still don't have the resolu-tion you sought, then try the tools and techniques I teach in my books and lectures: journaling, meditating, dream-analysis, intuitive divina-tion, and the like.

Because even in the postmodern era, we prefer to be proactive— to take matters in hand and get the job done as quickly as possible— in the West, as a culture, we have spent precious little time developing our capacity to be receptive. It takes a certain kind of faith to be willing to put things down and trust that somehow or some way, beyond your rational control, you will get the resolution you are looking for. But while in the West this capacity for stillness is underdeveloped, I had gone overboard. The books in my bag and the open doors up and down the professors' hallway held the promise of the balance I'd been seeking. After many years of learning how to quell my mind, it was time again to stir it up.

# 12

# *Philo-Semitism*

Just as I could not stuff even a single other book into my backpack, so was my mind being stretched to capacity. What I really needed to do was head back to my favorite cushy chair in the Div School library and close my eyes for half an hour, letting the swirl of thoughts settle down. I had still not selected my parable or text for Buttrick's sermon. I certainly could not proceed with my plan to write about the sowing of the seed. But I was not yet ready to get boxed into Jewish topics just because I happened to be born Jewish. The assignment was due in a few days and I would have to dig into the research and writing this afternoon or give up all hope of getting it done on time. But as I walked down the hall away from A.-J.'s office, heading toward the Divinity School library, I realized that Barr's door was now wide open. Office hour. There was no way I could tiptoe past without being seen. Despite my reluctance, I had no choice but to make my way down the hall.

"Carol! I'm so glad you came," Barr called out as he spotted me. His enthusiasm caught me off-guard.

"You asked to speak to me?"

"Yes. I wanted to apologize for what happened in class the other day. That was truly unfortunate. I want you to know that you are most welcome in my course. I have taken measures to ensure that such a thing doesn't happen again." *The enforcement of the policy concerning questions.* "In fact, I'd like to know. How is the course for you, aside from what happened the other day? Are you finding it interesting?"

This turn in the conversation took me by surprise. But it was easy to respond, since, in truth, I did find so much of the material we covered deeply fascinating.

"Very much so," I responded. "I had only been familiar with certain stories in the Hebrew Scriptures—the big ones, like Noah's Ark, Exodus, and the like. I had no idea how complex the scriptures really are, how much of it I had never read, let alone thought about. But Professor Barr, something puzzles me. When I told Marvin that I was pursuing my Masters of Theological Studies here, he told me Jews don't do theology. What did he mean by that?"

"Ah yes. It's a real problem, the word *theology*. While the word predates Christianity—its philological roots are actually Greek—there has been a history of individuals who call themselves Old Testament theologians, but who study the Hebrew Scriptures only in relation to the New Testament. The earlier literature devoted to Old Testament theology seldom gave any thought to what Jews might think about the matter. The major interest was to persuade Christians of the theological importance of the Old Testament, to provide a dominantly theological interpretation rather than a dominantly historical one, and thus to persuade them not to discount it or ignore it as part of their Christianity. The operation at times involved something of a 'Christianizing' of the Old Testament, and similarly sometimes involved disparaging remarks about Judaism. On the other hand, it often included high praise for the Hebrew mind and considerable insistence on the Jewish, rather than the Greek, mentality as basis for New Testament Christianity. But the terms of the discussion lay for the most part within Christianity. What Jews themselves might think about all this was seldom discussed. It is only relatively recently, around the 1960s, that something more began to be said about Jewish opinion. By the 1990s, a great deal more is being said. Christian writers in the field are increasingly keeping their minds open to the question of how their judgments in biblical theology will seem to a Jewish readership. The field of biblical theology has been one of the main forces tending toward philo-Semitism within twentieth-century Christianity."

"Philo-Semitism?"

"An admiration of the Hebrew mind and heritage—one of the major trends in theological circles today."

"But Jews don't do theology?" I asked, feeling a growing sense of embarrassment concerning the title, Masters of Theological Studies, I would be working so hard toward for the next three years.

"I was speaking here of one particular field, Old Testament Theology. If you are asking 'Are there any Jews who call themselves theologians?' the answer is yes. It was a term widely used in nineteenth-century Jewish liberalism. And there is a growing group of Jewish scholars today—though more prone to calling themselves Jewish thinkers than theologians—who are actively engaged in cross-religion conversations with Christians, Buddhists, and individuals of many faiths and traditions."

This last bit was not entirely new information to me, as among the many books stuffed into my burgeoning backpack was a paperback I'd picked up on a tip offered in passing by Lester at Cokesbury, the Div School's bookstore, not long after my less than heartening exchange with Marvin several weeks before. It was titled *Jewish Theology and Process Thought*, containing essays by both Christian writers and Jewish ones. Among the Jews represented were Harold S. Kushner, Rabbi Laureate of Temple Israel of Natick, Massachusetts, and Levi A. Olan, Rabbi of Temple Emanu-El, Dallas, as well as president of the Central Conference of American Rabbis. I had not the slightest notion as to what "process thought" meant at the time. But the fact that people like Kushner and Olan were willing to be publicly identified with the concept "Jewish theology" was some indication that perhaps "Jewish theologian" was not an oxymoron for which I should feel shame.

"The thing is, Professor Barr, that I don't care what you call it. I want to read the Hebrew Scriptures, to learn what various ancient and contemporary scholars think the many passages mean—Christian, Jew, Hindu, whoever. I want to be free to consider their particular insights or slants on the historical, mythological, and social contexts of the passages and then make up my own mind as to what I think the passage—or the Hebrew Scriptures as a whole—means to me. I want to enter into the conversation."

"Conversation with the text: that is the traditional Jewish approach. You see, whereas in the church the sacred text tends to be seen as a unified word demanding to be proclaimed, in Judaism the sacred text is seen as having many facets, each of which deserves attention. In addition to the Hebrew Scriptures, the Talmud and Midrash are essential for Jewish understanding of their tradition. Jewish Scholars like Jon D. Levenson emphasize the diversity of your texts and traditional understandings. Issues of covenant and promise dominate the Pentateuch, but they are missing from Proverbs, Qohelet, and the Song of Songs. The latter books, especially Proverbs, make no attempt to situate themselves within Israel's foundational story; they are unconcerned with the exodus, the revelation at Sinai, the promise and conquest of the land. But Jewish scholarship feels no apologetic need to concoct a 'unity.' Most of the Talmud is a debate, with majority and minority positions both preserved and often unmarked," Barr concluded.

I heard his comments, taking the time to think it through before I responded. At last, I replied: "But still, Professor Barr, or perhaps even, especially, there is some sense of what it means to be Jewish, some felt understanding that may perhaps be fed by scholarship, but that transcends all of it." I was thinking this through out loud. "In fact, maybe the central core of the sacred texts of Judaism and the Jewish tradition is this: the freedom to find meaning in diversity and to engage in the debate concerning the nature of God and the meaning of life."

I realized that, as I had been having my first in-depth encounter with the Hebrew Scriptures during Barr's course, I particularly liked the stories where God's own chose to struggle with their relationship to the divine. How many of the prophets begged God to call somebody else to deliver God's message to God's people? Jeremiah crying to God: "Why did I come forth from the womb to see toil and sorrow, and spend my days in shame?" So lonely was the prophet Elijah that at one point, he thought that he, alone in all the land, remained faithful to God. It took a divine revelation for him to be shown that there were seven thousand others who had likewise refused to bow down to the idol Baal. So distraught was Moses with his prophetic call that he begged God for help. "What shall I do unto this people? They are almost ready to stone me." I thought of Jacob wrestling with God at the banks of the Jabbok River, exacting from God after a night of combat his blessing. Abraham had the audacity to bargain with God, even to yell at God, when the occasion called for it. When God makes it known that he is going to destroy the city of Sodom, Abraham asks God to save it for fifty souls—then forty, thirty, twenty, then just ten. Ten righteous souls. Negotiating with God. Begging. Whining. It's like a real relationship. Not some idealized notion of remote, divine perfection, some God in the sky too distant to hear our complaints.

To honor complexity and paradox, and to resist the urge to reduce spirituality to terms small enough for the human mind to grasp: perhaps at the bottom of the Jewish well is the celebration of the mystery of God. In the depths of the mystery is the felt sense of being in relationship to a force so much greater than ourselves that we are reduced at once to trembling in awe before the divine, all the while trusting that God is with us, regardless of the circumstances with which we are faced.

"It has been enjoyable talking with you, Carol," Barr said, realizing that it was time for him to go to teach his graduate seminar on Fundamentalism. "I want you to know that you are welcome to come and talk with me about these things whenever you'd like. And, more importantly, I hope you will consider continuing your education and contributing your voice to the dialogue."

"You mean as a theologian? I'm going to have to think these things through. I don't want to have to be the only Jewish theologian in the world. Besides, I thought the only Jews whose opinions mattered on such things were the rabbis."

"Not at all," Barr assured me. "There are many, many Jews in the fields of historical-critical research, and many Jews who are devoted to discerning the meanings of Judaism's texts and traditions. Some are rabbis, of course. But many others have come up through academic routes. They hold professorships at Harvard and Oxford, at Claremont and at Emory. In fact, you'd be hard-pressed to find a religious or academic institution in this country offering courses in religion that doesn't have one or many Jews on the faculty. Perhaps you are not aware that there's a great demand in the universities for Jewish Studies programs? At a time when many religious scholars are having trouble finding jobs, individuals—Jewish and otherwise— with doctorates in Hebrew Scriptures and Jewish Studies are eagerly sought. Philo-Semitism is sweeping the academy. But, Carol, you should understand something. Whether you call yourself a Jewish theologian, or simply a Jewish thinker, I feel certain that you would be a welcome addition to the field."

As I got up to leave, my spirit soared with the compliment. After all, James Barr is one of the most respected Hebrew Scripture scholars in the world. That he even glimpsed the potential for me to play a role in the academy was deeply exciting to me. But a Jewish scholar? The thought was so remote from my experience of myself, I dismissed it out of hand. But secretly I realized with the tiniest of hidden thrills that even though I'd rejected the thought resoundingly, it had refused to go. Suddenly I knew what I would write my sermon on for Buttrick's class. Jacob struggling with God on the banks of the Jabbok River. With extra energy in my steps, I bounded out of the professors' realm and into the increasingly familiar ground of the Divinity School library.

# 13

## *Wrestling with Angels*

*And he rose up that night, and took his two wives, and his two hand-maids, and his eleven children and passed over the ford of the Jabbok. And he took them and sent them over the stream, and sent over that which he had. And Jacob was left alone; and there wrestled a man with him until the breaking of the day. And when he saw that he prevailed not against him, he touched the hollow of his thigh; and the hollow of Jacob's thigh was strained, as he wrestled with him. And he said: "Let me go, for the day breaketh." And he said: "I will not let thee go, except thou bless me." And he said unto him: "What is thy name?" And he said: "Jacob." And he said: "Thy name shall be no more Jacob, but Israel; for thou hast striven with God and with men, and hast prevailed."*

Genesis 32:22–28

On the way to my favorite chair in the library, I was intercept-ed by Marvin who interrupted his sorting through returned books to greet me with unexpected enthusiasm.

"I was thinking about your question about Jews and theology," Marvin whispered. "I realized that given where you are coming from, there is one Jewish thinker you really ought to read. His name is Rabbi Abraham Joshua Heschel. I don't buy into his halachic stuff. But he raises some great questions. For instance, in *A Passion for Truth,* he asks: What is the goal of faith? Is faith a demand to rise to God's requirements? Or the promise of comfort and peace? Heschel finds profound similarities between the Christian philosopher Søren

Kierkegaard and the eighteenth-century Jewish Hassidic rabbi known as the Kotzker. Here, let me show you."

I was astonished to see that Marvin had a stack of books set aside for me, all of them by or about Rabbi Abraham Joshua Heschel. There was *I Asked for Wonder, Man's Search for God, God's Search for Man,* and *No Man Is an Island,* a book of essays from religious, spiritual, and civil rights leaders from many traditions extolling Heschel's genius at reaching across institutional boundaries to initiate interfaith dialogue. I vaguely remembered the much-photographed image of Heschel as the Moses-like patriarch who often walked with Dr. Martin Luther King through the walls of fire of Birmingham and Selma, long gray hair and beard and prophetic robes. Marvin flipped through the pages. Look what he says in *A Passion for Truth* about the Kotzker: that in order to achieve greatness, the individual must—well, here:

> knock your head against the wall and break through all of your human limitations that block your relationship to God. To do so takes an incredible commitment to the Truth about yourself and your deepest motivations, for the tendency is always to do right and good in order to make yourself look good to God to get God's rewards rather than to do good for its own sake. In order to keep one's motivations pure, one must always be on the lookout for the performance of ritual by rote, "just because he did so yesterday." Because this is so difficult, humanity is bound to fall short of this goal. But sinners who know they sin are humble and God stays with them.

Marvin continued, gathering energy as he went. "This is not, however, a consolation that either the Kotzker or Kierkegaard indulged in themselves. Heschel says they saw faith as a demand rather than consolation. Here, look at this quote from Kierkegaard:

> Every individual ought to live in fear and trembling, and so too there is no established order which can do without fear and trembling. Fear and trembling signify that one is in process of becoming, and every individual, and the race as well, is or should be conscious of being in process of becoming. And fear and trembling signify that God exists—a fact which no man and no established order dare for an instant forget.

"And this one by Kotzker: 'It is dangerous to perform surgery on the soul—but man must live dangerously.'

"If I were to believe in God," Marvin continued, "that's the kind of God I would believe in. Not the milquetoast feel-good crap that oozes out of most of our religious institutions. Anyhow, I didn't want to leave you hanging. Here, take these and tell me what you think."

By now, not only was my backpack bulging to the bursting point, but my arms carried an equally abundant load of books. There were the books A.-J. had loaned me; the book on *Jewish Theology and Process Thought*; my textbooks for Barr's class, including the thick Oxford Bible; the Heschel books; and several other books I'd picked up along the way including *Jewish Renewal* by Michael Lerner, handed to me by Willow, who'd asked my opinion on it. I headed to my basement carrel, a tiny private room with locking desk, chair, and bookshelf. Just placing the books I had carried in there with me that day had nearly filled the shelf. I surveyed my treasures, feeling like King Midas in the counting room. And like King Midas, I felt my greed for more to be insatiable. If only I could have all the contents of all of these books in my brain right now! And not just these books, but suddenly I felt the urge to read traditional texts of Judaism. The Talmud and the Mishna, and the medieval commentaries of Maimonides, the Kabbalah and Moses Mendelssohn, Martin Buber and Sholom Aleichem, Theodor Herzl and the Zionists, and the contemporary writers too—Jewish thinkers like Emil Fackenheim, Will Herberg, Gershom Scholem, and Elie Wiesel!

An invisible barrier that had separated me from the Jewish tradition fell suddenly away as I sat trembling in awe and fear before the books, visible and not, that danced before my eyes. Humbly I surrendered to the discomfort of A.-J.'s confrontational questions, admitting to myself that not only had I rejected Judaism, but even more uncomfortable to admit, *I had rejected the religion before I really knew the religion.* Kotzker's words came back to me in full force. *"It is dangerous to perform surgery on the soul—but man must live dangerously."*

At last I was ready to take on Buttrick's assignment: to research and write my sermon on Jacob wrestling with man and God on the banks of the Jabbok River. I would carry out the procedure as I'd been taught this time, beginning my studies with the Christian theologians like Claus Westermann. But I would follow my Ariadne thread into the uncharted realms of Vanderbilt University Divinity School's Jewish Library, and there, for the first time in my life, seriously enter the world of Jewish commentary and thought, of Mishna and Talmud, of paradox and debate. *Man must live dangerously.*

I began my studies. Claus Westermann sees the receiving of the name "Israel" by Jacob to be the manipulative effort by later editors artificially to bolster Jacob's image as a patriach, dismissing all efforts of fellow exegetes to find spiritual meaning in the passage. And then there was St. Ambrose, who asserted that the numbness in Jacob's thigh as a result of the struggle "foretold the cross of Christ."

Slamming St. Ambrose shut, the time had come at last to step over the sacred threshhold. I walked quietly toward the wooden door to the Jewish library. As I opened the door to enter, I wondered what I would find inside. Would I be exalted by the knowledge of my own tradition—or repelled? Would my studies of the library's contents lead me closer or farther away from the religion to which I was born? Trusting in God as I had for many years and desiring, at last, to see if I could find a place for that trust within the community of my tradition, I plunged in.

My heart was beating rapidly as I opened the Jewish commentaries, from ancient times through contemporary ones, to read about Genesis 32 from the Jewish perspective. For once in my life, I did not have to reinterpret Chinese symbols into Western terms to which I could relate; I did not have to steel myself against the reading of Christ into Jacob's limp. All I had to do was be who I really am, reading the texts before me. As I read, it was as though the years of resentment and guilt, shame and righteous indignation were lifting off my back. In Jewish texts, I watched the rabbis debate who the "man" Jacob wrestled really was: angel or God? In *Judaism Magazine*, I contemplated a psychologist's interpretation of Jacob's limp as symbolizing his having finally achieved in his life a more considered and mature outlook. "Limping is a hesitating walk, symbolizing a slower, more mature consideration of learning how to deal without ruse or guile—and hopefully, with love." I resonated with this, but laughed out loud when the author went on to assert that the struggle on the banks of the Jabbok was a symbolic attempt to resolve a sexual conflict. "Jacob born circumcised never had to surrender to father. . . . What is missing from his life is a sense of mastery based on his own accomplishments." Huh?

But I was getting something out of all this, my heart and mind filling up with a sense of Jacob as he wrestled on the banks of the Jabbok River. At last, it was time to write. What did I think the passage meant? Each of the writers I'd read challenged me. I could keep that with which I resonated, discard the rest. What is the fear that keeps so many of us, on the one extreme, boxed into one tradition or another, unwilling to allow the fresh air of new ideas and challenges, even silly or dangerous ones, to sweep us to new levels of reflection and understanding? To struggle with the diversity, opening up one's heart to guidance toward the center, closer to the truth because it has been tested?

On the other extreme, why have so many of us ignored our own traditions entirely—the centuries and evolutions of thought that have already walked so many of the paths we must navigate before us— believing that we can discern the truth directly from God devoid of any intellectual scrutiny or preparation whatsoever? Are most of us looking for the easy way, the shortcut, to relationship to God, when what God is really calling us to do is, as the Kotzker writes, knock our heads against the wall in order to break through? Studying the many pages of notes before me, submitting them to intellectual scrutiny, following faithfully my own intuitions about what rang true or false, praying, meditating, scribbling, erasing, wrestling my heart and mind, my relationship to God, onto paper. That was the stuff of my first sermon, a sermon I was to find myself reading before Buttrick's class just a few days later.

# 14

# *Jacob at the Jabbok*

JACOB AT THE JABBOK: WRESTLING WITH GOD
AND WITH HUMANITY AT MIDLIFE
*A Sermon by Carol Orsborn*

Do you remember a best-selling book that came out several years ago called *The Imposter Syndrome?* It turns out that a number of apparently highly successful people live the entirety of their lives as if the rug were always about to be torn out from beneath their feet. They do not feel that their success has been earned and at every turn, they expect to be exposed as the frauds they suspect, in their heart of hearts, that they are.

That the book has sold so many copies tells us that there are a whole lot of us driven by the fear of exposure for being the flawed humans we know we really are. We work overtime keeping our acts together. Surrounded by the symbols of success, only we know how wide the discrepancy between the image we present to the world and how we feel about ourselves deep inside.

Such an imposter was Jacob, son of Isaac. You remember the story? How Jacob cleverly manipulated his brother Esau's birthright away from him? Then, sinking even more deeply into deceit, used a sheepskin to simulate the hair on his brother's arm in order to steal his brother's blessing from his blind and trusting father? But this is a dog-eat-dog world, right? And so Jacob took advantage of his opportunity, climbing the ladder of success. Over the years, he continued to play in the world of deception, taking turns being deceived by others and defrauding and betraying them right back. In other words, he was what we think of as a successful businessman. In fact, by the time Jacob hit midlife, he had built himself a large, attractive family, wealth, riches, position, and not just one wife, but two (not to mention their obliging female servants). Far away from the scornful memory of his father and Esau, he looked to the world like he had it all. But there was one thing all his clever manipulations had failed to bring him: peace of mind. Deep in his heart, he longed for a sense of legitimacy: to know that he, on his own, was worthy of God's blessing.

As so often happens in the Bible—not to mention our own lives, as long as we are asking the right questions and are willing to engage in the real struggles—the yearnings of his heart were about to be answered.

They were answered at a place called the Jabbok River, on the eastern border of what was someday to be called "Israel." Jacob had packed up his formidable treasures, his family, cattle, and worldly goods, and embarked on the arduous journey toward the home he had left so many years ago. Along the way, the small, rich caravan made a steep descent into the deep river gorge of the Jabbok. One can only imagine what was going through Jacob's mind as each and every step brought him closer and closer to the one he both dreaded and longed with all his heart to embrace: his brother, Esau.

Suffice it to say that by the time the descent was complete, it was darkest night. Something moved him to release his caravan, sending them away across the river into the darkness of the distant shore, while he remained behind. No children to distract him, heads of cattle to count, wives to entertain him. Utterly alone with himself in the darkness of night.

And in the quiet of the depths of the dark descent, he began to wrestle. All night long, he struggled with his past, his desire to dominate and control, his shame and his fear. He wrestled with the very roots of his deceit: the painful discrepancy we all feel from time to time between how we hope we are being seen by others and the more flawed versions we know ourselves to be.

The Bible portrays the lonely Jacob in a life-or-death struggle, wrestling through the night with a mysterious stranger. Live or die? the stranger demands of him. Is this the question of an angel, a demon, or of God? Choose death, continuing to use deceit and manipulation to keep up with the self-hatred of false appearances? Or somehow find it within himself to find out what it means to be more fully alive?

Eventually the sun rose, as it always does. The struggle ended at last, but not before Jacob understood how much his decision would cost him. He had chosen life. He, who had for so long and so recently sought to stride triumphant over others, had been left lame and exhausted, begging God for peace of mind. The key—for Jacob and for all of us who live our lives feeling that at any moment we could be exposed and shown to be wanting—is that he was willing to be broken. It was more important to face the truth about himself and to make the painful commitment to try to do better, even if that meant he could no longer keep up appearances. He had been forced to grapple with the despair of his own imperfect humanity, and yet he chose to go on. He had engaged in a struggle worthy of him.

And God blessed him there, "for I have seen God face to face, and my life is preserved."

There are two lessons we can take from the story of Jacob's struggle at the Jabbok River. The first is how important it is to take time alone, to stop the busyness and intrusions of your daily life from time to time, and allow the pain of your own internal dissonances to rise to the surface where you, too, can wrestle with the truth. Only when you face the truth, unarmed and vulnerable, can you see what needs to be changed and commit yourself to doing better in the future.

But there's a second lesson, too. For it says in the Bible that Jacob not only struggled with God but he struggled with man as well. Challenged by what the Bible is teaching us, I have come to believe that we are being guided by this story to forgive ourselves for our failings, for the imperfection of our humanity. Can you face the discrepancy between your ideals and your reality and yet find a way to live with vitality and commitment? This is the essential question those of us in midlife are forced to confront: How does one reconcile one's self to limitations, and yet find sufficient heart and hope to keep on trying for something better?

It was a newly humbled but deeply committed Jacob who at last limped across the Jabbok, fully prepared by his struggle in the night to face whatever lay ahead. For the point of this story is not that we never deceive others, make mistakes, get our values wrong. As human beings, we are all imposters exposed by the light of our own best intentions. The way to resolve the Imposter Syndrome is not to quell the dissonance by acting perfectly. But rather, it is to find within ourselves the strength and courage to struggle with and let ourselves be broken by the dark night of truth. Ironically, it is there, in our wounds, that we come to receive the most important blessing of all: the knowledge of what it means to be more fully alive.

My throat was dry as I waited for the class's response. "Very good start," Buttrick began as he and the doctoral students went to work on the differences between the mechanics of written and oral rhetorical logic and style. Before I even knew what the terms meant, I had crafted a narrative sermon. Some of the sentences were too long. Some more concrete, contemporary anecdotal illustrations of the points I was making would add punch. Don't ever begin a thought orally with the words "that" or "it." I didn't mind the feedback, even when as the class unfolded, several of the students began outdoing each other with increasingly sophisticated criticisms, keeping one eye on the manuscript before them and another on Buttrick to make sure he was noticing. But it wasn't anxiety about my writing style that made my throat go dry. It was—dare I use the word?—my theology. Would my interpretation not only pass muster within my own inner sensibilities of what is true but also resonate with a community of people who have studied the Hebrew Scriptures in depth?

I didn't have to wait long after class to get my answer. Lester was the first to arrive at my side.

"Great job, Carol. It was great to hear a Jewish interpretation of that passage. It was as if you were talking right to me. I don't know any ministers, myself, who don't sometimes wonder if they are frauds. The truth is, it takes a terrible toll on us to feel that we have to keep up some kind of act for our congregants. I'd really like to have the chance to talk with you more about this. I have the feeling you could help me with some of my own midlife issues."

"Of course, Lester. I'd be honored."

"Great. I was thinking of getting a prayer circle started with some of us here. We're getting going around Thanksgiving. The way a prayer circle works is that we get together once a week for an hour in the chapel, catching up with one another's spiritual stories. Then we do a little prayer and meditation. I think you might like it. You'd certainly add a lot to the group.

"By the way, as I said, your sermon was great. But I do have one suggestion. I think you should have continued the story on a bit, through the part where Jacob meets Esau on the other side of the river and they reconcile with one another. The way you have it right now, it's all about Jacob getting right with himself. That's part of that individualistic Age of Enlightenment stuff we were talking about the other day: the progress of humanity via the advancement of the individual. I don't deny that self-awareness and inner knowledge—forgiving yourself and the like—are important. But if I have read the Hebrew Scriptures correctly, the emphasis is not on personal growth per se but on serving the community. The prophets tell us in many ways and times that the individual must be willing to give up everything, even his or her own serenity, to carry out God's will. The scriptures, as I read them, are not really about peace of mind but, rather, about doing what is right for the greater good. If you continued the story, you'd bring Jacob around to the point of reconciliation with Esau. That way you could move the emphasis beyond his internal struggle and consummate his spirituality outwardly, with his relationship to others."

As usual, I was challenged by Lester's feedback. But something deep inside me resonated with his uncomfortable insight. Perhaps by joining his prayer circle, I would receive as much—comfortable or not—as I was prepared to give. I thanked Lester and asked him to let me know when the group was going to meet.

# 15

## The Prayer Circle

The chapel had turned out to be another safe haven for me at the Divinity School. A simple, sunny room with movable chairs, there was not a single cross or Jesus anywhere in the room. I could sneak in before a midterm and count on an hour or more of being undisturbed as I sat alone on the floor, eyes closed, calming myself down. This was the kind of spirituality I had learned in California. It was peaceful and safe. I could count on God to be there with me, and for many years that was all I thought I wanted or needed.

This time, however, I was not alone. In fact, I was in one of the chairs arranged in a circle, a single candle lit and set on the floor in the middle. Lester was there, of course, and so was Sammy. Emma walked in, greeting us all warmly. Then finally Willow, whom I'd asked Lester to invite, came to complete the circle.

"Welcome," Lester whispered, as we sat in silence for a few long moments. I must confess, I was breathing more shallowly than usual, nervous that what sounded to me like a mad dog panting would draw undue attention to myself. But nobody seemed to notice. Finally, Lester began.

"How it works is this. Each of us takes a moment or two to share the most pressing spiritual challenge that is up for you this week. We don't really get into dialogue or analysis. This is not psychology. This is about witnessing and support. As we continue through the weeks, we'll get a sense of each other and what God is calling each of us to do. Our intention is to create a community of faith."

Red flags flew, but it wasn't me who spoke next.

"Which faith, buddy boy?" Sammy chimed in.

"Not faith in the sense of this or that tradition. I know we have a Baptist, an atheist, and a Jew in our circle, an Episcopalian who is thinking about converting to Catholicism, and I am a minister with the African Methodist Church. The way that I can see us forming a community of faith is in our deeply held spiritual sense of being on a mutual quest for understanding. This group is about helping each of us advance in our personal relationship to God—and our relationship to the traditions that have formed us—in the company of others who feel likewise called. Does that work for you?"

"No Jesus?" I asked. Everyone chuckled.

"In terms of the prayers, we've got plenty of material to work with that will give us common ground without having to particularize in that way. Most of us here resonate to the Psalms, for example. But when we share our spiritual journeys with one another, we need to be free to use the language, the imagery, and our particular understanding of the truth—even if there are differences between us. If one of us says something the other dislikes, we need to learn how to discuss the conflicts respectfully. I hope we will learn how to allow each other to have different paths to what I personally believe will be the same end for us all—regardless of what we think it's going to be—letting many of our differences pass in order to focus, instead, on what it is that we share."

"Sounds good to me," I said quickly.

"Great. Who wants to go first?"

Sammy waved his cane in the air.

"I believe we have a volunteer. Sammy?"

"I'm thinking of dropping out." Sammy wasted no time with preliminaries.

"I can't stand it here. I'm really trying to get with the program, but I'm only finding out what I suspected for a long time. Religion is really out of it. What we need is governmental regulations not theology if we want to build a better society. I should have gone to law school."

"What makes you say that?" Emma asked.

"Take the story of Jacob stealing Esau's blessing from their father, Isaac. I've heard this thing discussed from morning until night until I'm good and sick of it. Was it right what Jacob did? Was it his sacred destiny if God wanted him to do it? Does the end justify the means?

What kind of a God would encourage deceit? What was the culture of the time's understanding of deceit? And so on and on and on. Nobody's even mentioned the real point of the story. All you future ministers and spiritual leaders trying so hard to get it right and you can't even see the nose on the end of your own face."

"What do you mean?" Emma asked.

"The point is what happened to Isaac. His son took advantage of his disability, and he gets blessed for it? And then you turn around, and you have all these conservative Christians working to cut funding for social services programs for the disabled. Rush Limbaugh, campers! Don't you get the connection? Throughout the Hebrew Scriptures and the New Testament, darkness—blindness—is seen as evil. Light—vision—is the metaphor for truth and goodness. This is bad, bad medicine."

"But surely you knew that story before you got here," Emma pressed. "My sense of the school so far is that we have carte blanche to critique the difficult parts of the material, to strip away the false and the troubling, in order to find our way to redeem the deeper spiritual truths that called us here in the first place."

"That's just it," Sammy replied. "I wasn't called here to redeem the deeper spiritual truths of my tradition."

"Then why did you come?"

"Because it was the only way I could get my dad to keep giving me money. He's still hoping I'll be a minister and take over his church when he retires. I'd rather die than do that, but I'd rather be here then working at some crappy job."

"Oh Sammy!' Willow cried. "I'm so, so sorry."

"Sorry?" Emma responded. "Maybe Sammy's father isn't blind, but Sammy is every bit as deceitful as Jacob!"

"Whoa!" Lester broke in. "This is not an encounter group. Look, this is meant to be a safe place for us all. Sammy, would it be fair to say that you are struggling with vocational issues right now: Is this the right place for you to get what you need in order to better address the issues of people with disabilities?"

"Yes."

"And that there are related issues, in terms of your relationship to your father and your own sense of integrity, that you are looking at?"

"Yes."

"Perfect. I have an idea. Would you mind all joining hands with Sammy for a moment." We joined hands and taking Lester's lead, bowed our heads.

"Gracious God, please be with our friend Sammy this week as he tackles these difficult issues. Let Sammy remember that he does not need to be alone in this and that he can call on you and on us for support. Amen."

"Did that feel all right, Sammy?" Lester asked.

"Yes. It was all right. But don't ever do that to me again!"

We all breathed together in quiet relief as Sammy emerged from the circle of hands, the color having returned to his cheeks.

Lester went next. He, too, confessed to having vocational difficulties. His further studies were putting an enormous financial and time strain on his family. In order to pay his tuition, he had been forced to take a job at the Divinity School bookstore on top of his full-time ministry. His wife wanted him to give it up and be content with his calling in the church and his respected position in the community. But Lester had become increasingly burdened with the sense of having to keep up a facade with his parishioners. How could he lead them spiritually when he, himself, was facing his own midlife crisis of meaninglessness? What was God calling him to do? Intuitively, he felt that school, the doctorate, was leading him toward resolution. He wanted to have an impact on his denomination at a leadership level, have a voice in updating the liturgy to make it more inclusive to women, for example. But the sacrifice was enormous, and the doubts that had set in, were even a greater burden. We prayed for Lester.

For Emma, things were not working out well in terms of her daughters. Her husband had decided that the separation wasn't enough. He was filing for divorce, going for sole custody of the kids in California, claiming that Emma's desire to go to Vanderbilt University Divinity School was proof of her flakiness. "Voluntary poverty" the court papers called it. He knew that in her denomination, women could not be ordained as full-fledged ministers. This was his proof that she had not truly been called to ministry and that this whole divinity school scheme was little more than a scam to defraud him of huge chunks of his salary. If she would drop out of school and take a job as a secretary, he would drop proceedings against her to regain control over the children. What was she to do? We prayed for Emma.

Willow had a happier story to tell. Thanks to me, she reported, she'd been introduced to Congregation Micah. In fact, she'd been attending Friday night services for over a month now. She'd never felt as welcomed anywhere in her life. She felt that she had come home.

My turn. What spiritual challenges were up for me this week? Willow had come home to my Judaism—and where was I? I'll tell you where I was, hacking my way through the underbrush of the Christian majority that was sending weedy tentacles into every aspect of my life. As Thanksgiving approached, the undercurrents of Jesus, Jesus, Jesus hummed to me on the many radio stations that in San Francisco would have been filled with affiliates of NPR. Here, the financial advice show was Christian-based. The talk-show hosts were conservative Christians. Grant and Jody both came home from their public school choirs with sheet music in hand to practice for their Thanksgiving concerts. Virtually every song: *"Praise Christ.* " Grant had made a nice friend, nice in every respect except one: he had made it his personal task to save Grant's soul. The last time his friend Mark had been to the house, he'd encouraged Grant to throw out his Dungeons and Dragons materials, along with some of the books on Eastern philosophy that I'd casually left lying on the coffee table. "It's too late to save myself," Mark exhorted Grant. "I've done so many bad things in my life, there's no hope for me. But you've still got a chance!"

I began to realize that unlike San Francisco, if we did not specifically do something proactively Jewish, the kids would get swallowed whole by the open-mouthed Jesus whale that swam these fervently Christian waters. They would not meet other Jewish children. They would not sing more than an occasional, begrudgingly token Jewish song. They would pass their adolescent years in communities that considered them to be, at best, a novelty; at worst, a target. Then one day my gentile husband, Dan, who had brought us to Nashville to further his career in the country music industry, came home quaking in anger. He'd gone to meet with a commercial jingle production company, thinking they would be a good client for his marketing firm. The first session had gone fine. But at the second meeting—the one in which contracts were to be signed—pen in hand, Dan had been asked by the president of the firm nonchalantly, as if in passing, whether or not he'd found Christ.

"Is that a condition of employment?" Dan asked, incredulously.

"Only if you want the business."

"Then my answer to you is this: it's none of your business. Work is one thing. My religious and spiritual beliefs are another. All you need to know from me is that I am a professional and that my ethics are aboveboard. How I get there is none of your concern."

"I hear you, buddy," the CEO responded. "But if you tell me two plus two equals five, I can tell you that's just fine with me. But you'd still be wrong."

Dan put down the still-capped pen and left. Watching our little family struggle to find safe haven in Nashville, a place where one sometimes wishes for the anonymity of a big city, a small enough place that community and spirituality and faith can be both a blessing and a problem, he had an idea. "Maybe we should join a temple," he suggested. "What do you think?"

What did I think? That was what was up for me this week. Willow, the Episcopalian, had found her way home to Judaism while I still wandered outside the temple walls. Join a temple?

# 16

# Rabbi's Chambers

And so it was that I found myself, twenty-four years after my departure from Judaism, back in a rabbi's chambers. This time it was an office in a former discotheque rather than in temporary space down the block from a delicatessen. I sat on the rabbi's comfortable sofa, waiting for him to get off the phone and turn his attention to me. I was sure he would be thrilled to find out that I was thinking about coming back. *Quite a catch,* I hummed to myself. But secretly, I steeled myself against the judgments of old memories: decisions around marrying out of my faith made in my youth, nurtured by life, and irretrievably part of my present and future. I had heard that Rabbi Kanter and the brand new Congregation Micah welcomed interfaith couples. More than that, I had heard that they thrived on diversity, honestly and enthusiastically embracing people of all races, sexual preferences, and economic classes who considered themselves to be Jewish and/or who were willing to commit themselves to making the attempt to live an authentically Jewish life. But who defined and determined what the nature of that life would be? Were there hidden agendas? My first impression of the temple—based on my ill-fated quest for God on Rosh Hashanah several months earlier, had been less than inspirational. We would soon see.

It was a smiling, open-handed rabbi, one part entertainer, one part Harvard scholar, who finally completed his call in order to hear my story. Kanter had majored in the arts at Harvard. In addition to pursuing his rabbinate at Hebrew Union College in Cincinnati, he had managed to write a book or two on the Jews of Tin Pan Alley. Even though he was recently appointed to Micah, his bookshelves were already overflowing with plaques, stuffed animals, and hand-made Jewish ornaments, tokens of the love and respect he'd gathered over the past several decades as he'd served his previous congregations and headed up numerous ethical, interfaith, and human rights com-missions around the state of Tennessee. People high up in both the Democratic and Republican parties had connections to Micah. And despite Kanter's vulnerable affability, he had, as I was soon to find out, a spine of steel.

"So what brings you here today?" he asked.

I leisurely told him my story, starting with my exile from North Shore Congregation Israel, my adventures in New Age spirituality, my fondness for Shabbos Shul, my struggles with Nashville and the Divinity School. In a final flourish, I described my quest on Rosh Hashanah and how let down I was by what I had hoped to find. Nevertheless, I was willing to give Micah a second chance.

When I finished, the rabbi's chambers were very, very quiet.

"Let me get this straight," the rabbi said at last. "You came to check our community out, passing judgment on us from one experi-ence, one of the least typical services of the entire calendar year, our ranks swelled with hundreds like you who have likewise not made a commitment to us. And you make a decision about whether God is or is not present for you on that basis?"

He looked at me with such a mixture of astonishment and pity that my inner hum concerning what a prize I would be for Judaism suddenly issued forth as a little, uncomfortable cough. He continued.

"We are a Jewish community, dedicated to bringing to life the words of the prophet Micah. To do justice, love mercy, and walk humbly with our God. That doesn't have to do with walking in cold off the street with the demand that we dance, chant, and whatever turns you on into God's presence. I'm very glad that you had that experience in San Francisco and that it kept you on the line for a more serious engagement with the religion to which you were born. But it's not what Congregation Micah is about. Judaism is not merely about what God will do for you. It's about your willingness to keep your agreements with God. You come here and make a commitment to us, to Judaism, to the Jewish people. You become a part of this commu-nity. You find opportunities to be merciful, to do justice, and to walk humbly amongst us, and then we will talk about God's presence in your life. If you are willing to accept these terms, then you will be welcome at Congregation Micah. We would love to have you, your husband, and your children join us."

I looked at the bookshelves, loaded with the tokens of love. They loomed huge above me as I shrank deeper into the cushions of the sofa wondering if I would ever find my way back to a place I could call home. I understood what Rabbi Kanter was saying to me. Something deep and forgotten resonated to the simplicity of his message. *To do justice, love mercy, and walk humbly with God.* But could I do this? My past route to God, dancing into a spiritual frenzy, forgetting my problems, and short-circuiting the demands of daily life to merge with divine spirit, seemed infinitely preferable. And yet, I had that in San Francisco, and it had loosed me from its grasp and sent me East. *It—* God. God had summoned me to Nashville, had called me to divinity school, had urged me to check out Congregation Micah, had walked me into Rabbi Kanter's chambers and into the depths of his cushions.

"Do I need to let you know right now?" the words finally formulated on my lips.

"Of course not. Take your time. Come visit with us on a Friday night or Saturday morning: tonight, if you'd like. Take some of our classes. Join us in some of our social events. Bring Dan and the kids. Have your kids visit Sunday school. Get to know us and let us get to know you."

The rabbi's secretary peeked through the door. "Rabbi, your next appointment just arrived."

"Are there any other questions?" I could tell he would stay with me as long as I felt unfinished. That could be a long, long time. Any other questions?

Okay. *How can you believe a God who acts in history and yet who lets the Holocaust happen?*

*Which is the holier approach: to pull away from the materialistic world in order to develop yourself spiritually—or to throw yourself into the world to transform it?*

*Are you born sinful and broken, and is the point of life to heal the rift between you and God—or are you born whole, and is the point to remember this?*

*Does faith in God's compassion make you passive? Can you use belief in an afterlife to neglect your responsibilities in this world?*

*If you no longer believe that God will avenge your enemies for you, but sends you events in your life, like illness or financial success, as punishment or reward and the like—is this maturing spirituality evidence of the evolution of your consciousness, or of the evolution of God?*

*Is religion about special knowledge or about finding God in the ordinary?* Instead, I simply asked: "What time are services?"

After that conversation, in the lull after midterms, I found myself listlessly leafing through nonpressing assignments from the safety of my divinity school library chair. My eyes kept wandering toward the wooden door that led into the Jewish library. In the haven of my reference room every whisper sounded like shouting. I kept reading the same paragraph over and over again. Finally, I bounded from my seat and swung open the portal, feeling my power like a gunslinger throwing wide the saloon door at high noon to face . . . what? To face the prophet Micah, that's what. I began pulling ancient texts from the shelves, blue covers with crinkly yellow paper that threatened to crumble in the exuberance of my quest. White covers with Hebrew and English text side by side, tiny commentary in type, pencil and pen scrawled up the sides and around the corners. I climbed inside the pages, through the text of Micah 6:1–3 and into a court of law.

> *Hear ye now what the Lord saith:*
> *Arise, contend thou before the mountains,*
> *And let the hills hear thy voice.*
> *Hear, O ye mountains, the LORD's controversy,*
> *And ye, enduring rocks, the foundations of the earth:*
> *For the LORD hath a controversy with His people,*
> *And He will plead with Israel.*
> *O My people, what have I done unto thee?*
> *And wherein have I wearied thee?*
> *Testify against Me.*

I, a good law-abiding citizen, was being summoned by the Hebrew Scriptures, to witness the trial of the millennium. The prosecuting attorney is calling the aggrieved party to the stand. And who is it that has been wronged? Walking toward the docket, engulfed in a cloud of holy smoke, a mountain or two as bodyguards, is none other than God. God begins. And as God does, the very hairs on the back of my neck stand at attention. For God is looking straight at me and calling me by name. Just moments ago, I believed myself to be safely protected in the comfort of my library chair. But now God is looking at me and crying these terrible words:

*"What have I done to you? What have I done that has allowed you to break your agreements with me?"*

It is I who stand accused by God.

In the Hebrew Scriptures, this is the setting for the delivery of God's message to Micah: God's call to do justice, to love mercy, and to walk humbly with thy God. The prophet Micah, commissioned by God, marches us before the judge, confronting us with our broken agreements. These words, reminders of what we have covenanted with God to do, are not warm and fuzzy. They are not simply slogans intended to make us feel good as we enter the temple gates. And neither is Judaism intended only and always to be warm and fuzzy. Judaism can also be God holding us accountable when we least expect it. Micah is not about our comfort: Micah is about our keeping our agreements with God, no matter how uncomfortable that may be.

At the heart of this is the reminder that when our forebears stood at the base of Mount Sinai, they made a binding agreement with God on behalf of all the generations of Jews to come. When I was born a Jew, I automatically entered into covenant with God. Covenant is a legal term. And when the prophet Micah describes a courtroom scene to remind us that we have made a covenant with God, we are reminded that we have entered into a legal agreement with the Divine. As in any legal agreement, once the services have been provided by one party, the other party must do as they've agreed, as well. In the Book of Micah's trial scene, God reminds us of everything God has done for us. God has given us life. God has given us the freedom to impact our own destinies. God has given us inspired texts and teachers to show us the way to live righteously. We accept these priceless services that God has offered to us. But here's the part we tend to forget: God expects something in return. And what is it that God wants? God wants us to be God's people, keeping God's commandments, holding ourselves accountable for doing what God requires of us. That is keeping our end of the agreement.

Now everybody knows it's easier to make agreements than it is to keep them. After all, God led us out of Egypt a long time ago. Certainly, we've got good excuses why, after all these years and all that has happened, we should be let off the hook. But then again, how about that queasiness we feel when we know we're not really doing what God requires of us? Not even we buy our own lame reasoning. Oh yes, indeed: God has that way of showing up at the most inconvenient times and in the most uncomfortable ways.

I felt a light tapping on my shoulder. So deep in thought was I, that the finger sent electric bolts through me. Willow stood there. Is it possible that such a slender finger could have punched such a wallop?

"Emma's had terrible news," Willow whispered. "Her husband won an injunction against her and she is being forced to return her girls to him in California."

It took me a moment to collect my thoughts.

"Is that possible?"

"She was served papers right in the middle of coffee hour! Where were you, anyway?"

"I was at Micah. Meeting with Rabbi Kanter. I'm thinking of joining."

"You are? How wonderful! Maybe we can go together next Friday night. But in the meanwhile, Emma needs our help. Without the kids, she can't afford her apartment. She needs us to box everything and move it to my place for now. We're pulling the prayer group together to help. It will take three or four hours next Friday afternoon."

Friday afternoon? Dan and I had planned to take a ride out to Bell Buckle, where rumor had it there was going to be a terrific little arts and crafts festival.

"Friday afternoon? Oh, I'm so sorry, Willow, but I've got something important to do I couldn't possibly change. But please, tell Emma if there's anything else . . ."

The librarian came over to us, reproach in her eyes. "The patrons are complaining," she whispered. Willow gave a sad, little wave and left me alone with my books.

God was looking straight at me, holding me accountable. And even then, even when cornered, I still looked for ways to justify my shortcomings, some way that wouldn't require too much of me. We live in a world of shortcuts. When we want the queasiness to go away, we hope there's something we can do to get it right with God again. Perhaps there was something else I could do, something that wouldn't cost quite so much. I'll send her my prayers. Give her the name of my lawyer. But Micah explains that keeping up our end of the agreement with God is not about what we think is a good idea. God does not want negotiations or gifts or bribes. What God requires of us now is what God has always required of us. And what is that? To do right by our fellow human beings. Imagine, a God who doesn't want gifts or bribes, but only that we be willing, if necessary, to sacrifice our personal comfort in favor of serving the needs of the greater community?

As I thought about the day's events, I really wasn't sure that this was something I was willing to do. Anyone who has a conscience, who has ever felt a nagging feeling in the pit of their stomach when they've done something they know is wrong, wants to know the answer to the question "How can I get it right with God?" The real question is whether once we have the answer, we will have the courage to sacrifice our comfort in order to do what God requires of us? That is the sacrifice God asks of us. The sacrifice Willow had asked me to make—and that I had refused. As much as I cried inwardly for community, for a return to a place called home, was I really willing to pay the price that being in community would exact from me?

# 17
# *Friday Night Services*

One of the most difficult parts in going to temple that first Sabbath was explaining to Jody that if she were asked her religion, she could no longer say "half Jewish, half Christian." As the daughter of a Jewish woman, due to the Jewish laws of matrilineal descent, she herself would be considered to be fully Jewish. But what other people considered her to be was not of the slightest interest to her. Even at ten years of age, she held the firm, unshakable conviction that her religious self-definition was her own—and solely her own—business.

"But Jody, you can't be half Christian and half Jewish because in order to be a Christian, you have to believe that Jesus Christ was the son of God sent by his Father to sacrifice his life for our sins in order that we be saved. If you don't believe that, then you're not Christian."

"If that's true," Dan piped in as we drove the tree-lined road across to the east side of town, "I know an awful lot of people who go to church, who really like what Jesus taught, who try to live by his values and examples, but who aren't Christians either."

"Anyway, that's not why I'm half Christian. I'm half Christian because I love my Daddy. And I'm half Jewish because I love my Mommy." That was Jody's conclusion and she was through with the discussion.

"I'm just saying that if you are asked your religion, you are Jewish. And if you say anything other than that, be prepared to have to defend yourself."

"Lay off her, Mom," Grant responded on his sister's behalf. "Jody can handle herself. But I'm a little worried about you."

It's true. Of the four of us, I was the only one who seemed to be undergoing rigorous psychological preparation for what was to come. Jody was mostly focused on the temple's promise of childcare, complete with Disney movies and board games. Dan, still suffering from the guilt of having moved us from the foggy expansiveness of San Francisco-style spirituality to the often-blinding glare of Good News that reflected off the buckle of the South's Bible Belt, trusted that anything that could possibly happen within the temple walls would be better than having to hear one or the other of us whining about that day's onslaught of Jesus' love. Grant, who'd been Bar Mitzvahed in the upbeat spirituality of Shabbos Shul several years previously, clearly considered himself to be Jewish. But steeped as he was in science fiction and martial arts, he did not prefer to think of ultimate causes as someone with a white beard sitting on a throne somewhere in the sky, Jewish or otherwise. In his spare moments, he was eagerly reading physics and philosophy books, fascinated by the possibility of a unifying theory: one overriding, consistent mathematical law of the universe that would explain everything.

The moment we walked through the doors of Congregation Micah, any concerns about being outsiders melted away in a wave of friendly handshakes and smiling faces. As Rabbi Kanter suggested, a routine Friday night service did give us a better sense of the true community. There were several hundred people gathered in the sanctuary, many of them chatting in fluid circles during the moments before the official start of services, greeting one another as the dear friends they had quickly become. The temple, founded just one year prior, had grown ten-fold. Some of these people had known each other all of their lives, but many were newcomers to Nashville. The Jewish community was astonished at the growth, particularly since—like researchers tagging wild, spawning salmon—the leadership of the Jewish Community Center, Hadassah, B'nai Brith, the various temples, and the like, had thought that they had a pretty good handle on each of Nashville's four thousand identified Jews. Where did all these new Jewish families come from? With a few painful exceptions, they weren't coming from the other congregations. Pencils flew to paper, and the realization dawned that the Jewish community was not four thousand, but probably six to eight thousand and climbing. The influx of Jews into Congregation Micah was being fueled by the large number of Jews flocking to Nashville to play leadership roles in the country music industry, and in the burgeoning health and medical professions. These were people involved one way or another with Vanderbilt University, as well as people coming from a rich underground of interfaith and interracial marriages and from other previously institutionally disenfranchised groups, such as gay men and women, who were attracted to the concept of the first new congregation to open in Nashville in over a hundred years.

Our family's arrival that Sabbath night was part of the first heady rush of confirmation that they were really onto something sweeping through Congregation Micah at that particular moment. It was becoming increasingly obvious that there was a pent-up demand in people who desired a Jewish life to find a way back into the institutional arena of Judaism. The hands that reached out to us that first Sabbath were there to pluck hearty survivors from the choppy waters of life outside community and into the warmth and stability of their extended family. This could be a place where I would not have to steel myself against an opening benediction dedicated to our savior, Jesus Christ. A place where people would understand that a matzoh ball is not some new piece of athletic equipment. Where I could be Jewish without having to explain why it was I did not wear a wig. As much as I missed the eclectic spirituality of San Francisco—the sense of freedom and fresh air that blew regularly through the vast expanses of my spiritual domain—there was something delicious about being greeted and hugged and seated simply on the basis of the shared assumption of our cultural and spiritual affinities. Was this what religion was like in the beginning? Before it became something you had to do just because your parents did it? A time, long ago and lost for many of us, when people reached out to one another as affirmation of our shared values? The arena within which to practice living out our highest aspirations in the company of others who were similarly inspired?

Having parked Jody in childcare, the three of us made our way up the aisle. "Carol!" I heard Willow's familiar high voice calling to me. "I saved you guys seats."

Willow! A cold bolt of shame shot down my spine as I realized that I had neglected to prepare Dan to lie about how we had spent the day, and that soon it would become apparent that I had not helped Emma move simply because Dan and I had instead gone to the crafts fair in Bell Buckle.

"You really missed it!" Willow whispered, as we settled into our seats. "Emma had forty boxes, mostly books. Not to mention her refrigerator and washing machine. It took us six hours!"

"Oh my gosh," I swallowed hard. "How's she doing?"

"She's pretty torn up about the kids going. It really felt good to be able to do something for her. But I stretched the ligaments in my leg. No big deal. It's just that I'm still a little weak from the injury that brought me home from South America. Oh well, it will heal."

I could tell that she was about to ask me how my day had gone, when Rabbi Kanter entered the bima and a welcome hush fell across the room. Never have I been more grateful to hear an opening benediction issue forth from a rabbi's mouth. Still burning from shame—in this of all places—I vowed to pay special attention this time to the words of the service, hoping to find redemption by allowing whatever meaning could possibly emerge out of the prayers and rituals to rise above the more mundane thoughts that had preoccupied me the last time I'd been in this room.

I was not fully successful. But there were moments. Our prayer book was *Gates of Prayer for Shabbat,* Shabbat Evening Service I. The service begins: "Source of mercy, continue Your loving care for us and our loved ones. . . . Keep us far from all shame, grief, and anguish; fill our homes with peace, light, and joy. O God, fountain of life, by Your light do we see light."

I rolled the words off my lips in English and in Hebrew, getting off to a good start allowing key words like *mercy, shame,* and *O God* to send their tender roots into my heart. But before they could fully take root, the congregation was singing *"L'cha Dodi"* to a tune pretty enough in its own right, but completely unfamiliar to me. Dan and I made a valiant effort to follow along, but when everybody else's voices went up, we found ourselves in the embarrassing position of having gone resolutely down. Grant shot an uncomfortable look at us, having at some point realized that his every move was being studied by several pretty teenagers across the aisle. Dan, Grant, and I stood proudly for the Sh'ma, grateful that we could each recall the watchwords of the Jewish faith: *"Sh'ma Yisrael: Adonai Eloheinu, Adonai Echad!"* But when we continued in English, I secretly took offense as my childhood rendering "Hear, O Israel, the Lord our God, the Lord is One" was blatantly mistranslated by the prayerbook to read "Hear, O Israel, the Eternal One is our God, the Eternal God alone!" How dare they change the words! When the congregation continued on to sing the Sh'ma, even the most sacred melody of my childhood had been unceremoniously replaced by an imposter.

And so it was that I wove in and out of the proceedings, consecutively swept up and dropped down as page turned to page. By the time we reached the familiar blessing over the bread and wine at the end, I was emotionally exhausted. Jody and the other younger children had been released from childcare and as congregants warmly kissed the cheeks of family, friends, and neighbors wishing each other "good Shabbos," she was tugging at me to take her to the sweets table in the rear of the sanctuary for the community gathering after services, the Oneg Shabbat.

As congregants and visitors nibbled, chatted, and hugged gaily, I realized that despite my personal exhaustion there was something worth exploring further here. Until this evening, I had never thought to ask myself where the prayers in the service had come from? Who wrote the music? Why were there changes from one service to another? I had always sort of assumed that God had written the music to the Sh'ma. Or maybe, it had been my first rabbi, Siskin, making up the harmonic progressions in his study.

However it was that we arrived at the particular words to say and songs to sing, perhaps Sabbath does work its special magic of mercy and peace. For by the time we'd nibbled through our cookies and fruit, both Willow and I had forgotten to return to the subject of how I'd spent my day. Instead—as Dan recognized a fellow music industry executive from the Row, excusing himself to say hello—Willow and I explored the questions this service had raised. She was taking Buttrick's introductory course: "Theological Foundations of Proclamation and Worship." And her first assignment had been to analyze the order and meaning of worship for the religious institution of her choice. She'd chosen Judaism, and she'd chosen the very service we'd read tonight. Would I like to read her paper? She promised to drop it off in my school mailbox—a square, wooden cubby in the common room—the next day. Meanwhile, Grant came up to us, beaming. The rabbi had asked him if he'd like to join the temple's first confirmation class. There were ten or so kids who'd already signed on. Grant nodded to the gaggle of lovely girls who kept their eyes on him as he reported that he had told the rabbi yes. Dan came up, slipping his acquaintance's card into his coat pocket. And then, as the crowd was beginning to thin out a bit, Jody popped up.

"Mommy! Somebody asked me if I was Jewish and I knew just what to say. I told them my mommy's Jewish, my daddy's Christian, and I believe in God. Wasn't that a good answer?"

"That was a very good answer," I replied.

# 18

# *Willow's Paper*

The moment I found Willow's paper in my box, I squirreled it away to my safe chair in the library. If my classmates were gossiping quietly at the next table, I took no notice. I read page after page of Willow's work, as I simultaneously confronted the sweet and sour of how little I knew of my own tradition's spiritual heritage while encountering the answers to lifelong questions I had not even yet thought to ask. It turns out that the Reform tradition's Friday night service is neither exactly the work of God, unchanged from the beginning of time, nor is it something made up out of thin air by twentieth-century rabbis. Rather, it is the blossoming of a spiritual essence that finds its roots in the earliest days of the Jewish tradition, developing organically over the centuries. When you scratch the surface of *Gates for Prayer for Shabbat,* you find within it all of Judaism's previous incarnations preserved in the order and the essence of the worship service. Just as important, you uncover all the issues, the tensions, the struggles, and at moments the resolutions that made Judaism a living, growing religion and the God of the Jews, a living God. The service we had used that Shabbat, service number 1, was actually but one of a number in the prayerbook, each one with a different emphasis or tone. They ranged from the traditional service number 1 to the mystical. There are services with an ethical emphasis, services aimed toward self-realization, services mostly in Hebrew, and others mostly in English. Each of them draws nourishment from the totality of Jewish tradition: from prophetic idealism to Hassidic joy, from rabbinic wisdom to Kabbalistic mystery, from medieval bards to ancient commentary.

Given that in rabbinical tradition it is taught that God's revelation to Moses at Mt. Sinai encompassed not only the Ten Commandments, but both the entire written and oral Torahs as well as all future teachings of the rabbis, it is possible to conceive of the Friday night service—even with its gender-sensitive terminology and radical departures from some aspects of traditional Jewish ritual—as divinely ordained. Even so, Willow's paper pointed out that neither the order nor content of the Jewish worship service, unlike the Christian tradition, had ever been codified by an official body of theologians bent on logic and symmetry, but rather sprang organically from the community, often in relation to external events in history. For instance, in 500 C.E., the Justinian Edict forbade rabbinical interpretation of the Torah—and so it was that poetry first came to be included in worship, using symbolic elements familiar to Jews, but that would cleverly evade their Roman censors.

As I had experienced the previous Friday night, the service begins with the lighting of the Sabbath candles and a supplication to the "Source of Mercy." Now I read in Willow's paper that the opening prayer was formulated by a rabbi in 1891, the era of mass immigration to our country by the Eastern European Jews. Willow went on to point out that from the very beginning, the congregation's faith in God is assumed. The opening prayer does not ask for help in believing in God; neither does God ask his people to believe in him in order to be saved. Rather, there is a pre-existing basis of understanding, implied by the history of the covenant, that because God is merciful and honors agreements with the Jewish people, congregants can assume that a loving relationship is already present and continuing. When the congregation responds: "Keep us far from all shame, grief, and anguish," we are affirming that on this sacred day of the week, we can count on getting a foretaste of the Messiah's promise of the world to come. There is no place for shame, grief, or anguish on the Sabbath. Therefore, unlike weekly Christian services, there is no requirement for confession or absolution. On the Sabbath, the Jews are already unified with God. While there are other occasions, notably Yom Kippur, where Jews have the opportunity to feel their imperfection and ask God for forgiveness, on Sabbath, according to tradition, the Jew experiences only God's love.

As is the custom, the mother of the family says the prayer over the candles. Sabbath is closely associated with a feminine spiritual aspect: the organic capacity to create and nurture through quiet, receptive, inner processes. Sabbath is the seventh day of creation, the day of rest. Set in contrast to the busy routines of our everyday lives, Sabbath is a time for letting go and receiving divine inspiration and blessing. Lit at sunset to mark the beginning of a new day—which, in the biblical tradition, begins at sundown rather than sunrise—the candle initiation of Sabbath ritually symbolizes the fact that God has brought us out of the darkness of slavery to the light of freedom, where such a blessing as a day of rest is possible.

At this point, the service enters the first of three major prayer units, an order of service called *Kabbalat Shabbat* (Welcoming Sabbath), already fixed by the first century C.E. The first portion begins with six psalms, introduced into the service by a sixteenth-century Kabbalist mystic, representing the six days of creation leading to Shabbat. The psalms begin by offering thanksgiving for creation, emphasizing God as creator of the physical universe—specifically such natural phenomenon as the depths of the earth, mountain peaks, sea and dry land, and ultimately "Your people and Your flock." There is even one psalm among the group, Psalm 92, that the Midrash claims to have been the very psalm that Adam recited on his first Sabbath.

"It is a good thing to give thanks unto the Lord, and to sing praises unto Thy name . . ."

It is during the second psalm that the official call to worship takes place: "Sing a new song to God," the rabbi cries out. The congregation responds: "All the earth sing to the Eternal One!" Almost immediately, the psalm goes on to declare that the Eternal One is "far above the gods that are worshipped!" Legend has it that this early reference to other gods goes back to the generation following Christ, when those who considered Jesus to be the Messiah still considered themselves to be Jews, believing themselves to have the right to worship at the Jerusalem Temple. One explanation of the reference to other gods is that the Pharisees wanted to sniff out the heretics, watching carefully to see who refrained from saying it so as to evict them before the Torah was read.

As the congregation approaches the emotional climax of this portion of the service, the recitation of the Sh'ma, the rabbi leads the singing of *L'cha Dodi*. The song that had been unfamiliar to me turns out to have been taken from the first lines of the Kabbalist poem: "Beloved, come to meet the bride; beloved, come to greet Shabbat." In a tradition that has been lost to Reform Judaism, our ancestors dressed in white on Sabbath eve, going to the city limits together to greet the Sabbath. Can you imagine the power contained within the history of this weekly ritual?

Reaching this point of the contemporary worship service, the rabbi bids all to rise for the Reader's Kaddish: the Aramaic word for "Holy." The Kaddish contains no reference to death but rather, in keeping with the overall spirit of Sabbath, to a messianic age where death will be overcome. By now, the congregation is walking together through holy gates, the sacred Sh'ma preceded and followed by a set of two benedictions praising God: four being a number of mystical meaning in the ancient Hebraic tradition.

At last we have arrived at the Sh'ma, the affirmation of the fundamental Jewish belief in unity: that there is one God and that it is humanity's task to search out the goodness of creation with one's whole being. The achievement of unity—the reconciliation of contradictions and the overcoming of conflict, perceiving and becoming aligned with the perfection of God's creation—constitutes the fundamental human task, according to Judaism.

The next major section of the Jewish worship service is called *T'filah*. During the *T'filah*, having thoroughly considered the creation of the physical universe, we are brought to consider the completion of God's work: the meaning of the seventh day and, to the best of human ability (which is to say, with great humility and awe) of the nature of God's being. These quiet prayers—as are all the prayers in the Shabbat service—are communal prayers. On Sabbath it is deemed inappropriate to turn our thoughts to our own private needs. On this special day in which God has "given us our souls back," we are assumed to be transfixed in such a state of fulfillment that our problems are not even on our minds. For this taste of peace, the congregation offers its thanksgiving, responded to by the rabbi's "Priestly Benediction," inspired by an eleventh-century rabbinic tradition. This is followed by silent prayer, in which each of us is urged to enjoy experiencing the nearness of God.

The final portion of the service features the rabbi's sermon, based on the week's Torah portion, concluding with a benediction that traditionally summarizes the high points of the service for the benefit of latecomers. The ark is opened, a brief adoration and joyous hymn of thanksgiving is offered, followed by the rabbi's messianic supplication for a time when God's name shall be worshipped in all the earth. This is not so much a climax as an ebbing away, as the congregation sings a final hymn before the rabbi eases effortlessly from liturgy to announcements of coming events, followed immediately by the blessing over the bread and wine. In one hour, we have made our way from creation to revelation, to redemption, and to divine providence. We have expressed gratitude for God's role and relationship with us, and we have affirmed the acceptance of responsibility that such a relationship entails.

While many of the elements in the service have been passed to us through the ages unchanged, Judaism is a dynamic religion, responsive to the needs of ages and circumstances. This is exemplified by the many forms that God takes in the Hebrew Scriptures, at times accessible, at times shrouded in mystery, but never predictable, set, or staid. At the Red Sea, God appeared as a young hero. At Sinai, God was an elderly judge. Willow quoted from Jewish scholar Arthur Green's essay "God, Prayer, and Religious Language." He says: "Each revelation was in accord with the need of the hour. In the day of battle, a frail, elderly God could hardly be the right vision for the moment." Green goes on to point out that this does not mean that religion was "made up" by people to fulfill their own psychological needs, but, rather, that God is willing to appear to us in our moments of need in forms appropriate to the time and the individuals.

The prophetic model was one that encouraged Jews to question the prevailing conceptions of God and to mine deeper spiritual ground in search of an authentic, personal relationship with God. Judaism has always encouraged theological revision as historical situations demanded. Many people regard this prophetic revisionism as the key to the ongoing vitality of Judaism, enabling it to survive against great odds over the millennia. This largely accounts for the development and toleration of such a wide variety of Jewish prayer-books and traditions. Green writes: "Jewish law, insofar as it remains a significant guide in this area, is rather open with regard to what is truly required in prayer. Maimonides concludes that the recital of the Sh'ma and the spontaneous prayer of the heart are biblically ordained obligations and that all other liturgy has the lesser status of rabbinic ordinance." Green writes that he "could readily conceive of a Jewish community in our age in which twice-daily prayer, at sunrise and sunset, consisting of a period of meditation to be concluded with a communal calling out of the one line Sh'ma. That is a synagogue I would like to attend sometimes."

The latitude Jews have in worship is further underlined by the fact that since the second century C.E., we have been involved in an ongoing debate concerning just exactly how binding rabbinical law should be. This was the century in which the fall of the Temple in Jerusalem brought down with it the Temple's specially ordained priesthood. In their absence, spiritual leadership and guidance fell to lay teachers, "teacher" being the closest English translation of the Hebrew word *rabbi*. With competing schools and philosophies, each rabbi was free to interpret the law and the tradition as he felt best. The emphasis in the religion fell from a formal priesthood into the possibility of encountering holiness within each individual heart. This freedom of worship is underlined by the traditional Jewish teaching that there are not one, but thirty-two secret routes to God. Additionally, in every generation, tradition teaches that there are thirty-six righteous people—tzaddiks—whom God considers to be sufficiently spiritually adept to justify the creation and continuance of the entire human race. These thirty-six individuals are anonymous and unidentified during their lifetime. Just as for centuries rabbis were unwilling to accept money for their spiritual services—earning their living instead by such trades as carpentry and shoemaking—Jewish mythology abounds with stories of tradespeople who appeared to pass their lives in menial labor. Only after their deaths was the brilliance of their minds and spirits uncovered in the form of dusty documents stored beneath workbenches and straw beds in remote country villages. After the fall of the Temple, God no longer resided in any one place, but became a mobile God, able to manifest wherever and in whomever there arose the desire to pray.

The Hassidic master Rebbe Mendel of Kotzk inspired Martin Buber with this simple story.

"Where is the dwelling of God?" So asked the Rebbe of Kotzk of a number of learned men who came to visit him. They laughed in surprise. "What a thing to ask! Is not the whole world full of His glory?" Then the Rebbe answered his own question. *"God dwells wherever man lets Him in."*

I couldn't wait to talk with Willow about her paper. I found her in the common room, thumbing through the school newspaper. I knew she wouldn't mind being disturbed.

"Your paper is incredible! I had no idea how progressive Judaism is," I began. "It's not something written in stone handed down to us for us to follow. I see now that it is an organic, living tradition with plenty of room for people like you and me to play. The question is, what are the limits? How far can one press the boundaries of Judaism, or any religion, and still be embraced by the tradition?"

"Don't you think it has to do with intention?" Willow responded. "As I understand it, the essence of Judaism is the willingness to make the attempt to fulfill our agreement with God, the willingness, even, to sacrifice our self-interest and comfort in order to serve our fellow human beings."

"That could be a good test. If you are making changes in your spiritual practice only to achieve personal joy and peace, individual freedom can easily become self-indulgent. But if you want to know whether your prayer life is truly effective or not, you need only ask if you have emerged more aware of and willing to sacrifice your own comfort in order to carry out what God is asking of you."

Jews throughout the centuries have lived in the uncomfortable tension of believing that unity is possible, while existing in a world that has not yet been redeemed. As a result of Willow's paper and our conversation, I was beginning to understand that my spiritual life, including, or perhaps even especially because of, the discomfort I had experienced over the past decades, had been more fully embraced by my tradition than I had known. Was it possible that God had been operating in my life from the beginning, even when I felt estranged from Judaism and had embarked on my studies of other spiritual disciplines and religions? Had God not only been with me, but actually been initiating the impulse to explore beyond the boundaries of my faith tradition in order to return someday renewed and revitalized? *Menucha* is the Hebrew word that describes the spontaneous experience of the in-breaking of God, imbuing life with meaning and harmony. It is this *menucha* that encompasses the essential definition of what it means to be Jewish: the ability to envision one's reconciliation with God, one's fellow human beings, and one's own internal conflicts into one unity. This holistic experience of the Divine is the essence of Jewish prayer, an experience which I believe contains the key to the renewal of our tradition. As we sat there together in the common room, I felt for the first time that I was not a deserter, a refugee, but a part of the continuing history of the Jewish people.

# 19

# *The Monastery in Kentucky*

I could not wait for the prayer group to officially begin before giving Sammy my good news. I would have preferred to share my excitement with Willow, but she had not yet arrived to the circle of chairs Lester had set up for us in the chapel.

"We're joining Congregation Micah!" I crowed to him.

"Traitors!" he replied, without missing a beat, but with a forgiving trace of humor.

"Traitors? What are you talking about?"

"I thought you were one of us," Sammy answered. "You know, the great unwashed, set adrift from our fathers' religions, to explore the uncharted expanses of the great unknown, unburdened by the unnecessary baggage of the past."

"You sound like Marx," Lester chimed in.

"Groucho or Karl?" Sammy retorted.

"Who says I'm going to be burdened by old baggage, Sammy? I believe I'm strong enough to get back involved with Judaism and still retain my sense of adventure and individuality."

"Yeah, right!" His sarcasm, always quick and ready, had a more bitter ring than usual. We were passing time, waiting for Emma and Willow to arrive. "You think you've got them, but they've got you. You're going under, Berkeley. Your fellow hippies are crying from their graves. The thing is, we need to throw all religions out and start over again. That's our only hope."

"What's with him?" Emma asked as she took her seat.

"It's your father's church, isn't it?" Lester suggested. "Do you mind if I tell the group about it?"

Sammy nodded assent.

"You all remember that Sammy grew up in the church that his father heads up. Well, all of Sammy's life, the head of the youth group was William, a fellow that everybody adored. The guy wouldn't harm the hair on a mouse's head. So here's the deal. Somehow, word got out that William is gay. And Sammy's dad just fired him."

"Fired him without even a day's notice! Wham—just like that," Sammy took over the story. "I've made a decision," he paused hesitantly. "I'd like to wait until Willow gets here. Has anybody seen Willow, by the way? She didn't show up to read for me today."

"She wasn't in class this morning," Emma volunteered.

"Why don't you go ahead and take your turn, Sammy? When Willow comes, we'll catch her up."

"Okay. I've decided to tell my father that I'm not going to take over his church. In fact, I'm going to tell him that what I want to do is go to law school."

"God, Sammy. That's big. How do you feel about your decision?" I asked.

"Scared. But I know it's the right thing for me to do. I'm planning on finishing the year, though. It wouldn't be right to abandon my fellow campers when the fun is just starting!"

We spoke for a few moments, offering Sammy our encouragement and support in preparation for what we suspected would be a very challenging conversation with his dad.

It was Emma's turn. She was incredibly grateful to the group for the support they'd given her with her move. I cringed inwardly, but nobody noticed and, thankfully, neither did anybody say anything about my absence. Emma continued. She missed the kids terribly, but with the group's love and assistance felt that she had turned a spiritual and emotional corner. It was the first time she had experienced unconditional love. The group had come to her aid, asking nothing in return. It was a life-changing experience for her. But what was next for her, pressing her to move on as best as she could, was her upcoming interview with her ordination committee. She knew that they would be placing conditions on her ordination—that as a woman, she concentrate on leading Bible Study groups, along with other youth and adult education activities, rather than pastoring her own church.

"Even if I were willing to do that, it's their thinking that bothers me," she told the group.

"They truly believe that God created women in secondary status to men. They even had the audacity to cite the first Adam and Eve story to me, that darn rib thing. I tried to point out that there's a second version of the story, but they didn't want to hear it. So that's their explanation for why they won't give me a church. I know they're going to ask me next week if I agree or not. If I do, I'll be ordained with the conditions attached. But if I don't, they might very well boot me from the program. Will you guys help me pray for clarity—and to do what's right?"

We joined hands in prayer, stretching uncomfortably across Willow's still empty chair.

Lester reported that because one of his sons had knocked out a tooth at football practice, he was going to have to take a fourth job to pay the bill. He was already falling behind in his schoolwork, and this just might take him under.

"Join the club!" Sammy snorted. "Willow sure picked a terrible time to take a vacation. I really needed her help reading today. Where is that woman, anyway?"

Where was Willow?

At that moment, we heard rapid footsteps down the hall and we all turned expectantly toward the opening door. But it wasn't Willow who entered. It was Jered. His face was flushed red. Jered wasn't even in the prayer group, but here he was.

"Have you heard about Willow?"

The plaintive tone in his voice grabbed at my heart.

"She was mugged last night, coming home from her field education placement at the shelter. She was alone, in the worst part of town! And someone jumped her and stole her purse. The worst thing is, it knocked her down on her bum leg. She's on crutches."

"Crutches? Where is she now—at Vanderbilt Hospital?" Lester asked.

"Last night she was, the ER. But they let her go."

"Where is she now?"

"Her roommate drove her to a monastery in Kentucky this morning."

"A monastery in Kentucky?"

"She left a note for you all. Here."

"Prayer Circle," Lester read. "I'm so sorry I can't be with you today. Please know that I'm all right and that you have my love and my prayers. When I've healed, I will be back. In the meantime, I'm very worried about Sammy. Will one of you please take over my reading hours with him until I return?"

We sat there, speechless.

"Why Willow?" I asked at last.

"Why anybody?" Sammy replied.

"I mean, Sammy, that Willow is so good and loving. She doesn't deserve this."

"Deserve?"

"Why would God—" I tried to continue, but Sammy cut me off.

"—do this to somebody as good as Willow? As if God cares. Why did God make me blind? I'll tell you what my father's church would say. For punishment. For my sins. Is that what you'd like to believe? That Willow is being punished by God for what happened to her?"

"I didn't say that," I replied defensively.

"But that's the implication of your kind of thinking. That you believe in a God who ought to reward good people with good things, and bad people with bad ones. Then everybody gets all bent out of shape when something bad happens to a good person, or something good happens to a bad one. But check it out, Carol. Knock knock: the Holocaust, Carol? Or do you believe, like my people do, that all those Jews were chosen by God, all right—chosen to die because of their obstinacy in refusing to accept Jesus as their Savior?" Sammy was fuming.

"Back off, Sammy, " Lester said. "We're all upset about Willow. Look, the issues you're raising are big ones. Issues that every one of us has to struggle with. But the hour's almost over, and it's way more than we can bite off today. Here's what I propose we do. Jered, you're from Kentucky. Can you get a phone number for the monastery? I'll call up there and see if there's anything we can do to help. Carol, I can see you're upset. As a first year student, you haven't had time to explore the issue of theodicy in depth yet. But you might want to check in the Jewish library where the post-Holocaust literature is. I think you might find it helpful. And now, Willow's request. I would love to read for Sammy, but with the fourth job—"

"There's no need, Lester. I'll do it." All eyes turned to the voice that had spoken. Was there a touch of astonishment? Despite myself, before I could think through what I was doing—the hours of personal time I would have to give up in order to take Willow's place, the fact that he had just been yelling at me—I had volunteered.

"That's settled then."

We joined hands for our final prayer, but my mind had already left the room heading toward the Jewish library where I fervently hoped I would find cooler waters of wisdom with which to quench the burning in my soul. It didn't take long for my body to follow. I entered the gates of the Divinity School library, where Marvin, as was often the case, stood guard.

"How's it going?" he asked amiably. "Have you dug into Heschel yet?"

"No. As much as I'd like to. With the semester coming to a close, I'm still behind in my assigned readings. And now, I've got this burning need to read some of the post-Holocaust Jewish literature. Do you have any suggestions?"

"Heschel."

"Really?"

"Absolutely. Heschel was part of the third wave of Jewish thinkers who rose to the surface in the mid-1950s, along with Will Herberg and Emil Fackenheim. You might not agree with everything they say, but you've got to give them credit for trying to come up with a revitalized notion of the Divine in the wake of the Holocaust."

I thought this over for a moment, grasping a slick, silvery fin at last of the essential question that had been eluding me, perhaps all of my life: "How is it possible to believe in a potent Jewish God after the Holocaust?"

"Exactly. For hundreds of years, traditional Judaism based its conception of the Divine on the medieval Jewish philosopher Maimonides's notion of God as changeless, omnipresent, unlimited, and omnipotent. This is what Maimonides meant when he recited the Sh'ma: God is One. God, the all-powerful, who is in complete control of the universe and of history. Many Orthodox Jews still believe that destiny is entirely in God's hands and that when bad things happen, it is punishment for our transgressions. You will find books in the Jewish library twenty feet away from us by some of these Jews, ascribing the Holocaust to God's displeasure with the liberal Jews of Germany who dared to question the laws and rituals of Jewish Orthodoxy."

"Was Heschel one of the liberal Jews?"

"No. Here's how it goes. The rationalists of the Enlightenment were enraged by exactly the kind of thinking that would allow an Orthodox Jew to blame liberal Jews for the Holocaust. They thought of the Maimonides kind of God as nothing more than superstition—magic—choosing to place their faith, instead, in the essential rationality of humanity. They truly believed that the particularities of religion—one God over another—actually held humanity back from universal brotherhood. That if the Jews could shed their backward and separative rituals and ways, the enlightened goodwill of like-minded people of other religious traditions would prevail. People, stripped of their differences, would establish the Kingdom of Heaven on Earth. But it didn't work out that way. When the Nazis came to power, the liberals' faith in the essential goodness and rationality of humanity was dashed to the rocks, laying the groundwork for the next wave of Jewish thinkers. There were those who rose from the ashes of the Holocaust to declare that 'God is Dead'—a stance that departed on moral grounds from Maimonides's concept of an unwaveringly just God, but that had no better notion of God to propose in its place."

"So where does Heschel fit in?"

"Heschel came up through an alternate Jewish route, drawing his wellspring of faith from an ongoing mystic strand in Judaism, sometimes coexisting with, sometimes independent, from the mainstream tradition. While Heschel was an Orthodox Jew, he believed that his, and every individual Jew's, relationship to God was the key to Judaism's viability. In many ways, Heschel is a bridge between classical Judaism and those of us who have been struggling to retrieve a spiritual notion of God without the outdated ideological and social baggage of some aspects of our tradition's past. Heschel stood up in the midst of the Death of God movement to reaffirm a potent, spiritual God worthy of our reverence. At the same time, he insisted on a full involvement with the world at large, reaching out beyond the boundaries of institutional Judaism in interfaith dialogue and action. Both of these stances are consistent with the kind of God Heschel experienced. Do you still have the books I picked for you? I really suggest that you start with one of them."

I began my reading that day, with *Man's Quest for God*. Despite the fact that term papers were coming due, final exam review sessions being lined up by helpful teaching assistants, I continued to read. For a half-hour in the morning, before the family got up. Over lunch. In the few minutes before Barr walked through the door. After studying. Sometimes at night Dan gently would remove the book from my hand, placing it on the nightstand and turning off the light. As word came down from Kentucky that Willow was doing fine—choosing to take incompletes she could finish up next semester, rather than prematurely interrupt her spiritual, physical, and emotional healing at the monastery—I continued to read. *God in Search of Man*. As Lester looked increasingly haggard balancing the demands of his complicated life, I read on. Reading Heschel was my balm, my antidote. I rounded a corner and found Emma in tears. "It's nothing," she said. "Happens to me all the time. It will pass." I read *I Asked for Wonder*. I showed up for my reading sessions with Sammy who spent the time talking about his anger with his father instead of completing his research. Through final exams, through hugs and good-byes, through the winter break, I read Heschel. *A Passion for Truth. No Man Is an Island*. And as I witnessed Rabbi Heschel alternately circle, caress, evade, and claim a relationship with God for himself, so did I begin to dance, wrestle, retreat, and advance in the general direction of my own Jewish understanding of God: one that I knew must hold, not only before the trials of my own family and friends but also before the life-long-held images of children burning in the fires of Auschwitz's ovens.

## 20

# *Heschel's God*

*I have been wrestling with the problem all my life as to whether I really mean God when I pray to Him, whether I have even succeeded in knowing what I am talking about and whom I am talking to.*

—Rabbi Abraham Joshua Heschel

When Abraham Joshua Heschel considers what he really means when he talks both to and about God, he must begin by sharing the traditional Jewish understanding that God is neither a concept nor an image that can be grasped by the human mind. *"By the ineffable we mean that aspect of reality which by its very nature lies beyond our comprehension, and is acknowledged by the mind to be beyond the scope of the mind."** Long before one can even begin to approach the subject of thinking about God, the spiritual Jew senses God's presence. In Heschel's words, God is alternately a "pulse of wonder," "the source of Joy," and "pure presence." More often than not, this presence is felt not in abstract intellectual terms, such as the Greek's ideal of goodness or perfection, but in specific acts of compassion.

Because God is a concept that is beyond the grasp of the human mind, Jews are traditionally warned away from trying to capture

---

* The quotations from Abraham Joshua Heschel in this chapter are taken from three of his books, *God in Search of Man, I Asked for Wonder,* and *Man's Quest for God.* Information about them may be found at the back of this book in the section "For Further Study."

the sense or experience of God in images. Over and over, the Torah describes God as dwelling in "deep darkness" or descending to earth veiled in thick clouds. His name must be concealed, as in Isaiah, where even the Seraphim hide God's glory from their eyes with their wings. In Jewish tradition, there are no physical representations of supreme reality. The closest physical symbol we get is the empty chair for Elijah at the rite of circumcision and the open door at Passover.

The irony of the Jewish concept is simply this: the God we can conceptualize is not God, but a mind-made substitute. *"He who is wisest of God knows that he is most ignorant of His essence: while he who does not know Him, claims to know His essence."* To be wise, one need only ask the question: Who created the world? Heschel points out that we cannot answer this by referring to any cause or power, since the question would yet remain, Who created that power or cause? Inevitably, our pursuit ends with the mystery of creation.

So ultimate is God's power that the miracle of existence is only possible through the continuing action of God. If he were to remove himself for a moment, everything in the universe "would return to their natural state, which is nothingness." This is not to imply, however, that God designed the universe as a vehicle by which to share his essence. God and the universe are two essentially incomparable entities. To speak of God primarily as a designer of natural laws, order, and creation is to reduce God to something our minds can grasp. Heschel contends that it is far more honest to admit that we do not comprehend the origin of the universe and to sacrifice our intellects to silent worship of the mystery of creation, life, and history. The very act of our existence pays testimony to the ultimate.

Even in the midst of silence, Heschel cautions against a shallow understanding of the word *mystery:* *"We do not mean any particularly esoteric quality that may be revealed to the initiated, but the essential mystery of being as being, the nature of being as God's creation out of nothing, and, therefore, something which stands beyond the scope of human comprehension."* Heschel explains that the concept of mystery is nothing new. To the pagan eye, the mystery of life was death, oblivion, a demonic blind force. Pagans sacrificed to this dark demon, hoping to stave off hunger, illness, and misfortune. What was revolutionary in the Jewish concept was that behind the mystery lay ethical meaning: a God of righteousness acting in the world. In Judaism, what is mysterious to us is not mysterious to God. In fact, Heschel explains, God is the revealer of mystery. And what God reveals is this: God is not arbitrary, does not violate justice nor righteousness, and is eternally meaningful.

Given that Rabbi Heschel barely escaped the ovens of Auschwitz and lived to witness the destruction of the world he once knew, such an assertion is not to be taken lightly. Heschel explains his remarkable faith on the basis of his experience of God as being alive and in process. To Heschel, God is not a "thing" fulfilling orders for individuals on their terms according to their finite wills and consciousness. Rather, God places each of us in the perspective of the widest possible horizons, ranging beyond the span of individual lives, or even the life of a nation, a generation, or an era. The individual does not stand alone before God but as part of a community through space and over time. *"We are endowed with the consciousness of being involved in a history that transcends time and its specious glories. We are taught to feel the knots of life in which the trivial is intertwined with the sublime. . . . Our blossoms may be crushed, but we are upheld by the faith that comes from the core of our roots,"* Heschel writes.

Heschel explains his remarkable faith on the basis of his experience of God as being alive and in covenantal relationship with humanity. Humanity can be in relation to God, whether or not we understand fully how the mechanics of the relationship work. Through our relationship to our community, we sense the Divine within the mundane. God comes to us, not as a concept or a thing, but as an expression of life imbued with righteousness and meaning as revealed through events happening in time. While God remains mysterious to us, how it is we are to live with God is spelled out very clearly in the Torah. The heart of Heschel's theology is that the Jew is hereby asked by God to take a leap of action rather than a leap of thought. The Torah makes it clear that God is concerned that we fulfill his will on earth—and that the means of fulfilling his will is through our deeds. In return, in the end of days, evil will be conquered by the One. *"But in historic times, evils must be conquered one by one."*

Citing passages in the Hebrew Scriptures in which prophets and patriarchs wrestle with God, Heschel contends that an authentic Jewish life requires utmost courage and honesty including confrontation with God, when the occasion calls for it. This is a highly relational notion of God, positing a living, dynamic divine presence that can change and grow in relationship to creation while maintaining an eternal, ever-present essence. The Torah's many stories make it clear that God does not care about our comfort, but, rather, that we do God's will. This requires our stripping away our ego's selfish concerns, our tendencies to protect ourselves from an honest engagement with the issues, situations, and questions that impose themselves upon us, begging for us to respond with courage. We do God's will only when we become willing to be truth-tellers—to unveil our weighty fantasies, to warn against our nihilistic tendencies, to strip away our false understandings of God and of meaning down to the barest bone. We must become willing to struggle with the big questions, to huddle naked and alone in the shadow of the mystery, to submit our fondest notions to scrutiny. We must even, or perhaps especially, be willing to confront God with our utmost authenticity. God prefers our honesty to our arrogance; our questions to our dogmas; our righteous anger to childlike acceptance. Heschel points out that our tradition honors tzaddiks, holy people, who have moral power to which even God is willing to respond, like Abraham bargaining with God for ten righteous Jewish lives in the town of Sodom. *"The refusal to accept the harshness of God's ways in the name of His love is an authentic form of prayer,"* writes Heschel.

God needs us not only to adore him, but to be responsive to his will, to be fully alive human beings, commited to serving God. The responsibility is awesome. God calls us to right the wrongs of the world to the fullest extent possible. We are to be humble, generous, just, and kind. But often, a shadow is cast by our shortcomings and weaknesses. The less spiritually aware may content themselves with worldly considerations as compensation for discomfort. But for someone with the spiritual sensitivities of Rabbi Heschel, the self-awareness of the discrepancy between aspiration and reality is excruciating. And so it is that Heschel describes his own perpetual spiritual state as one of "endless tension" between adoration and dread. *"Every morning I pray. . . . But then, I ask myself: Have I got a right to take my refuge*

*in Him? To drink of His stream of His delights? To expect Him to con-*
*tinue His kindness? But God wants me to be close to Him. . . . It is an act*
*of God, falling in love with His people."*

In the very presumptuousness of having entered into covenant with
God, Heschel portrays himself as standing naked before the ultimate,
feeling shame and embarrassment for his everyday complaints. While
Heschel trusts always that the human soul is clean, he writes that within it resides a power for an evil *"strange god that seeks constantly to get the*
*upper hand over man,"* and if God did not help Heschel, he could not
resist it. Heschel sets the standard for us, struggling for inner purity, to
do good not with the hope of external reward or for egotistically stroked
feelings of righteousness, but for its own sake. He exhorts himself, as he
advises us, to pray not to praise or petition God, not to satisfy an emotional need, but to raise ourselves to a higher level of living. Heschel
gives the example of Rabbi Akiba who died while being tortured at
Roman hands. As he was being tortured, he recited the Sh'ma. With his
last breath, the word *echad* was yet on his lips. Tradition has it that at
that moment, a heavenly voice issued forth and announced: *"Happy art*
*thou, Rabbi Akiba, that thy soul went out with the word* echad."

Faith, our trust in God, is the expression of our connection to the
highest realm, the realm of the ultimate. We reach this connection
through our sense of awe, dread, and wonder: a state in which we fall
into awestruck silence or burst out in songs of utter adoration.
Through prayer, we regain a sense of the mystery that animates all
beings. *"Prayer is our humble answer to the inconceivable surprise of liv-*
*ing,"* Heschel exclaims. Just as prayer—raising ourselves to a higher
relationship to God—is an end in itself, so are wonder and amaze-
ment ends in themselves. In our experience of the sublime, we are not
engaged in a thing or a quality, but rather we are gifted with the in-
breaking of God. That this happens rarely is not a sign of personal
failure, for Heschel contends that the fully emancipated human being
is yet to emerge. In the meantime, we find ourselves as spiritual beings
constantly wavering, first soaring and then descending. At the peak,
we feel connected to unity with God. In the valley, we feel isolated
behind the thick screen of our own shadows.

That is why Halachah—ritual—is so important. By building routines and order into our everyday lives, we provide opportunities for

ourselves to place our thoughts onto God and away from our everyday, ego-driven concerns. Even when we do not become conscious of our connection to God, ritual and prayer remind us that we have entered into a covenant with God that remains valid regardless of how we happen to feel at any particular moment. We don't always, as individuals, live in the mystery. But through our liturgy, we do have access to those individuals and moments where the in-breaking of God has occurred in time as well as in space. Moreover, there exists always the possibility that God will seek us out, wherever we may find ourselves, in whatever state. God has the capacity to break through even to those who do not care for him. God is merciful and seeks out the weak as surely as the strong. It is the glorious paradox of God that one so infinite and boundless could care so intimately for finite human beings. *"There are moments in which, to use a Talmudic phrase, heaven and earth kiss each other."*

As the winter break ended, I closed the final book of the stack Marvin had selected for me. I knew Heschel's God was big enough to contain me: not only my joy and peace, but also my struggles. Heschel had put into words my sense that God had been with me from my earliest memories, sustained me through my mistakes and shortcuts, blessed me with eternal optimism, and given me a meaningful community that I could not, no matter how hard I'd tried, leave behind. Because Heschel's quest for God not only includes but also honors paradox, struggle, self-doubt, and unresolvable questions, so could mine. His faith may be illogical, it may waver, it may at one time inspire him to soar and at the next moment dash him on the rocks quivering in shame before God, yet none of this excludes him from God's loving embrace. Heschel teaches that his God—my God—prefers honest struggle to self-serving duty. In the past, when I adopted various spiritual philosophies in order to find neat resolutions I always came to a point where I felt the answers weren't big enough. Where I once thought of the paradoxes as confusing and unhelpful, I now recognized in them the honesty and integrity of my own tradition. How ironic that what I'd been looking for all these years was embraced and generated within the religion to which I had been born.

PART TWO

*Second Semester*

## 21

# A.-J.'s Class

Winter break covered such a long span of time, by the end, I had begun to wonder if my first semester at the Divinity School had been nothing more than a dream. As I approached the common room at the start of the new semester, I worried that my community of classmates had been an illusion. Even though I'd found myself thinking about Willow often over break, we had not known each other long enough to be deeply bonded. The same was true of my relationships with Sammy, Emma, Marvin, and Lester—and these were the closest of my companions. As vulnerable as we'd been with one another last semester, I realized with some degree of pain that I had neither called nor been called by any one of them over winter break. We had not exchanged cards or gifts. Then, too, I listened to a tiny voice in the back of my mind warning me that at its best, this community would be temporary. This semester I would have new teachers and new configurations of classmates. Some would have graduated from the Monday–Wednesday–Friday of introductory-level classes to the Tuesday–Thursday schedule for the more advanced ones and would disappear from my daily life. If his dissertation went as planned, Lester would be leaving at the end of the semester. The rest of us would be sorted out in two or three years to various denominations, callings, and regions of the world. As I walked down the long hall that smelled freshly of Lysol and chalk, I was acutely aware of how many people I had not yet gotten to know. I smiled gamely at pleasant faces, wondering if they could tell how removed I felt. I was happy to be back, but nervous that I had been making this all up out of my hunger for community.

Such dark thoughts soon dissipated in the bright sun of Willow's enthusiastic greeting. She got up from her favorite common room sofa to give me a hug, her limp noticeable to me for the first time.

"How are you, Willow! Gosh, we were worried about you."

"I'm fine, Carol. In fact, I've never been better. But I am concerned about what you are going to think of me."

"Whatever do you mean, Willow?"

"Carol, while I was at the monastery, I had a vision. As I lay there on my bed in my cell, Mother Mary appeared to me. And I realized that she was Jewish—the same way my grandmother was Jewish. It was a kind of unity, a full circle, in which I understood what these past few months have all been about. I've been being prepared to understand and accept Jesus at a whole deeper level. Carol, I finally know what I am meant to do. It wasn't just the better missionary program that was attracting me to Catholicism. It's the ritual identification with Jesus, the change of the wafer and wine into the body and blood of Jesus. I can feel Jesus in and with me now in a way I can't explain. I am planning to convert formally. I've already talked to my mother's childhood priest about it, and he's setting me up on a schedule. Carol, I hope you can find it in your heart to be happy for me. I am so grateful to you for the time we spent together at Micah. In fact, I still plan on going sometimes. When I go to temple, I feel so close to Jesus. Do you understand?"

Willow beamed at me, a beatific glow emanating from her fragile features. The truth is, I felt betrayed. But where and how does one go about navigating such intensely complicated terrain? I could not be angry with Willow. But feeling strangely, sadly used, neither could I fake enthusiasm. I choose my words carefully.

"Can you help me understand, Willow? Aside from the missionary work, what does Catholicism give you that Judaism doesn't?" I asked.

"Part of it is philosophical. Part of it is my personal experience. But they're interrelated. It's kind of hard to put into words."

"Start with the philosophical then. What happened after the mugging?"

"I had a lot of time to think at the monastery. Remember the book I loaned you? Michael Lerner's book, *Jewish Renewal?* You never told me what you thought of the book, but it had a profound effect on me.

Lerner explained that the core Jewish message is the belief that there is an ultimate power, greater than ourselves, that charges each of us as individuals to act on the belief that the world can be fundamentally transformed for the better. The Jews believe that evil can be overcome on earth. That was how Jesus related to his mission and that was the basis upon which I tried to act in the world."

"You make it sound past-tense. Don't you believe that any more?"

"After the mugging, I realized that I had taken too much on myself. I am just a human being. It would take a spirit like Jesus to really live up to the Jewish mandate. I realized that if I, a mere mortal, keep trying to take on the oppressive social structures of our society on my own, I'm going to kill myself. And that's when it hit me. Jesus sacrificed himself—gave himself over to the suffering—so that we human beings wouldn't have to take it all on ourselves. Because of what Jesus did, I can just do what I can do."

"Willow, it sounds to me like you've given up."

"No, not given up. Given over. That's the experiential part. The sense of being forgiven by Jesus for my inadequacies. There just weren't enough opportunities at your Friday night services to vent my brokenness. I really admire Jews like you who can stay positive and active in the world without needing somebody like Jesus to share the burden of your suffering. But while I was at the monastery, embraced by the incense and rituals, the holy statues of Mary, Jesus, and the saints, thinking about communion, reciting the rosary, I trusted that there would be a time and a place where I would feel whole again."

"South America?"

"Not South America, Carol. Heaven."

"And in the meantime?"

"I'm still planning on going to South America, but this time I won't be there alone."

"I see." My feelings tumbled head over heels in my stomach, too complex to sort through in the few minutes before class. Maybe there was some way for me to debate her and change her mind. But was that the right thing to do? I cared for Willow and I trusted that God was there for her, just as God was there for me. I didn't have to fix this right now—even if this needed fixing, which I wasn't sure was the case. And so as my classmates began sweeping past us toward our nine o'clock classes, I gave her a supportive hug and joined the flow.

I soon found myself in a large, well-lit downstairs classroom, the location of Buttrick's popular course, "Introduction to Homiletics." Unlike the doctoral-level course I had taken with Buttrick last semester, I would be taking this course with many of the first year students. Emma set herself down to my right, Jered just behind. I was eager to tell Emma all about Willow's extraordinary confession, but before I could, Jered leaned over to stage-whisper to both of us: "Did you hear about Sammy?"

"Is he okay?" Emma asked.

"Maybe. No. I don't know. His roommate just told me that over break, when he told his dad that he wanted to switch to law school, his father threatened to put him in a psychiatric hospital for evaluation. Sammy resisted. But now his parents don't know where he is, and he hasn't shown up back here yet, either."

"Oh my God!" I exclaimed. Professor Buttrick, watching the final stragglers wander to their seats, realized that the time had come to call the class together. He checked his portable alarm clock, and after comparing the time on the dial with the various extremes on people's watches throughout the room, decided that the happy moment had come at last.

"It's wonderful to see you all back here after the winter break," he began. "This semester we will be exploring just exactly what you mean when you believe yourself to be called to speak the word of God. "

Throughout the semester we would be writing and presenting a series of sermons, he explained. We could pick whatever passages from the Hebrew Scriptures or New Testament we would like to consider. "You, of course," he said looking at me, "are free to do all of your work within the Hebrew Scriptures." There were only a few new faces in this class who took notice of this special attention. For everybody else, having come like me from Barr's course, my Judaism was old news. If we were a village, I was the village Jew, a role I was becoming more and more comfortable with as the months unrolled. During the course of this second semester, we would each have the opportunity to present two of our sermons before the class. Were there any volunteers to go first?"

Jered's hand shot up.

Fine. And who will go the following week? And the week after? And so on and on until we each had our slots.

After class, Jered, Emma, and I walked together across the hall to the even larger classroom, where Professor A.-J. Levine would shortly be holding court. In just one semester, her reputation for both brilliance and drama had spread throughout the school and into the community. In addition to the Divinity School students, there were doctoral candidates, undergraduates, auditors, and special students—including more than a few working ministers—settling into the classroom seats, the wooden kind with arms widened and bent. Both Willow and Sammy were on my mind as I settled in for the opening lecture. But nothing, not even worry for a good friend, could survive what was to come.

Professor Levine, not so much dressed as enveloped in a fluffy pale blue and white sweater outfit, grandly removed her impossibly high-heeled shoes and began to lecture. She was trained as a ballroom dancer, and the quickness of her bare footsteps was exceeded only by her deft turn with facts and details. Between memorized citations of scripture, she rushed to the board to inscribe our minds with Aramaic, Greek, Latin, or Hebraic translations. As fast as we wrote, we could not keep up, grateful for those infrequent intervals when someone would sneeze. Only then would A.-J. interrupt her onslaught of knowledge long enough to bestow an elaborate "bless you" before moving on, giving us time to catch up with her rapid-fire thoughts. A historian of New Testament times by trade, A.-J. was also adept at linguistic, psychological, sociological, and theological issues—and more. The order of the course, we came to quickly understand, would begin by comparing and contrasting the four Gospels: four different versions of the Jesus story, each coming from different people or groups, in response to different cultural, political, social, and theological agendas of different times.

While I complained to my Christian classmates over the subsequent several classes that having never before read the New Testament I was overwhelmed by the profusion of new information that flooded over me, they gave me little sympathy. For having read the New Testament through their denominations' perspectives all of their lives, they had the formidable task of undoing their faith understandings in the light of historical thinking. Their sacred book, which had hung together so nicely as one seamless story about the birth, ministry, crucifixion, and resurrection of Jesus Christ, due largely to the wizardry of on-site editing by inspired pastors, not to mention an epic Cecil B. DeMille-magnitude movie or two, turned out to contain four different versions, not only of Christ's life, but also of the meaning of Christianity.

Take, for example, the case of the Messianic Secret. In all four Gospels, Jesus repeats to his followers that they are not to tell what they've heard or seen about him in relation to whether or not he is the Messiah. They are to keep his messiahhood a secret. In the Gospels of Mark and Matthew, when Peter guesses that Jesus is the Messiah, he is told by Jesus not to pass it on. But there's a difference between even these two Gospels. In Matthew, Peter's guess that Jesus is the Messiah is positively affirmed by Jesus: He is the Messiah. In Mark, it is not: Peter's guess is left unanswered. Along with pointing out such discrepancies, Professor Levine discussed possible theories of explanation. For instance, on a practical, social level, the Messianic Secret may have proved useful to early Christians as an explanation as to why so many Jews chose not to follow Jesus. In the earliest of the Gospels, Mark, written by someone who came to his belief in Jesus from outside the mainstream of Judaism, such explanations to his fellow gentiles may have been necessary. Why didn't more of the Jews, Jesus' own people, choose to follow Jesus? Why had missionary efforts turned largely away from trying to convince Jews that Jesus was the Messiah to focus instead on gentiles? The Messianic Secret put forth the explanation that the reason the Jews didn't follow Christ is quite simply that they didn't know Jesus was the Messiah. It had been kept a secret from them by divine mandate. Their obstinacy was part of the sacred plan. Surely this was a more palatable explanation than that they knew who Jesus thought he was—and simply did not buy his story. Of all the Gospels, Mark plays up the Messianic Secret the most.

But there are other implications, as well, played up or down in this and subsequent Gospels, depending on the various external and internal forces at work at any given time. Again, why did Jesus in one Gospel affirm that he is the Messiah and in another, refuse to answer the question? Is it possible that Jesus knew himself to be the Messiah but really didn't want his followers to tell because as a Davidic heir, he was a political threat to the Roman powers? On the other hand, is it possible that when Jesus in Mark fails to affirm Peter's guess of his messiahship, it is because Jesus really did not consider himself to be the Messiah? There are many other discrepancies, as well. Most of the Christians in the class had never studied the Gospels' accounts of the crucifixion and resurrection of Jesus side by side. When they did, they discovered contradictions ranging from the time that Jesus was crucified (Mark says 9 A.M.; John says noon) to Jesus's last words on the cross ("My God, my God, why has thou forsaken me?" reports Matthew. "It is finished," reports John). Jesus prophesied that he would be in the tomb for three days and three nights (Matthew). How many days and nights was Jesus actually in the tomb? Matthew, Mark, and Luke: three days and two nights. John: two days and two nights. Does Mary touch Jesus after the resurrection? Matthew and Paul: Yes. "They came and held him by the feet, and worshipped him." John: No. Jesus said to her, "Touch me not." And so on and on.

And then there are theological discrepancies. How to explain why Jesus, embodying love for the neighbor as he does, refuses to heal the Canaanite woman simply because she is not Jewish? She must grovel at his feet like a dog in order to gain his attention. And how do we explain Jesus Christ, the Prince of Peace, proclaiming "Think not that I am come to send peace on earth: I came not to send peace, but a sword." And finally, there are morally questionable citations, such as Mark's bold contention that for those who believe and are baptized "if they drink any deadly thing, it shall not hurt them." How many times must we read headlines of mass suicides by cults who have taken this text seriously?

Because I had no particular investment in the New Testament, such thought-provoking revelations struck me on a continuum ranging from mildly interesting to deeply exciting. The fact that Jesus may not have thought of himself as the Messiah, for instance, opened up all kinds of questions concerning the nature of Jesus' teaching versus what his followers and subsequent generations did to his message and story—possibly exploiting the work of one heck of a great rabbi, fully in keeping with the prophetic tradition in Judaism, to gather power and influence for their own agendas.

Many of the Christians in the class, however, were on a whole other continuum altogether, ranging from mild upset to near total devastation. Jered raised his hand tentatively one day, a plaintive note in his voice with which many in the room resonated: "If the Gospels can't get their story straight about Jesus' resurrection, then who are we to believe? And if we can't believe any one or the other, then what if it's not true? And if it's not true, if Christ did not die for our sins and get resurrected for our salvation, then why be Christian?"

Professor Levine handled such questions with great sensitivity and tact. Over and over again, she would say: "Just because there are discrepancies between the narratives does not mean you can't still choose what to believe. It's simply that you will now be able to have your beliefs informed by a more complete picture. You can be educated and faithful."

Even though A.-J. was Jewish, her office was often overflowing with Christian students who wanted to talk with her about their issues of faith. If they were sincere both in their quest for education and their quest for faith, they often emerged from their sessions with A.-J. with spirits rekindled. Even as I dipped in and out, often with a moist hanky in hand, to grapple with issues from the Jewish tradition, so did they enter her sanctuary convinced—as was I—that God gave us our minds as well as our hearts. Even if it looked grim along the way from time to time, ultimately things would fall back together in such a way that both our traditions and our scholarship would make sense.

But there were some who avoided her office at all costs, who felt that her facts, while indisputable, were somehow being framed within a suspiciously Jewish agenda, despite the fact that A.-J.'s historical inquiry was situated well within the work of the mainstream of Christian New Testament scholars. Jered, despite our bad start, was not in this category, although several of his co-denominationalists were. Jered had proven himself to be sincere in his efforts to tackle head-on the prejudices to which he had been born, spending many hours in both Levine's and Buttrick's offices. They were hard but productive hours, and Jered was slowly developing a reputation around the school as someone targeted for a leadership role in his denomination. He might just make an enormous difference for the good someday. But it was sometimes a long and bumpy road.

I avoided Jered when he was with his fundamentalist gaggle of student ministers, but my desire to check on the latest news about Sammy overrode my good sense. I carried my tray of soup and tea to his table in the refectory and asked if I could join him and his friends. They were so intensely engaged in conversation, they barely noticed my presence, sipping quietly at the end of the table.

"But Jews are like that," one of them was saying. "They are pushy and stubborn, and you can't trust them."

Oh, my God. Here we go again. I put my soup spoon down and was about to speak, when Jered caught my eye. I could see him grow in stature as he took this opportunity to right a wrong.

"Not all Jews," he said. "Hey, Carol's a Jew and she's not like one of those other Jews."

The group paused, took me in, thinking about what Jered said. But before they could respond, Jered was continuing: "Hey guys. The God Squad's practicing today at five. We've got a game with the business school Thursday. Who's in?"

Apparently disaster had been averted. The group had gone on to hoops and strategies as I, invisibly, worked at my soup. But the flavor had gone out of it. It was bad enough that I, who had begun to take the Divinity School's philo-Semitism for granted, had stumbled into the muddier waters of prejudice against Jews. I had yet to assimilate Willow's defection to Catholicism. And now it felt like the stakes were being raised yet again. For even worse than what these others were saying about the Jews, I realized with a sickening feeling in my stomach, was what I had done when I let Jered's artful dodge of dividing Jews into good ones and bad ones stand. In fact, all of my life, I had been doing pretty much the same. As I thought back to my first conversation with A.-J.—the one in which she described her response to the accusation that the Jews had killed Christ—I realized that despite my conscious sense that anti-Semitism was a subject I had not been confronted with in my sheltered life as a Jew, the truth was somewhat different. The truth is that I had never really before questioned whether the Jews had killed Jesus or not, I had not made peace with this accusation against my own people. I had simply taken refuge in the self-protective stance that if they had, at least I was not one of those Jews.

I remember one conversation, since coming to the Divinity School, when I was asked point-blank how I felt about the Jews in Jesus' time, and I glibly answered: "If I were Jesus, I wouldn't have liked those Jews either." With my Christian name and eclectic spirituality, I had a serviceable place in which to hide. But it sure as heck made the soup taste terrible. The guys were gathering up their trays, and still I remained silent. They left me sitting alone. And in their places were the ghosts of all those Jews I'd denied. Did I have more in common with these bigoted classmates than I had with my own people? I swallowed hard, vowing not to run away from this but to take it head on. What did I mean when I allowed the notion to stand unchallenged that I was not one of those Jews? But where to start? I remembered, then, that A.-J. had implanted the idea in me during our session together to go to the library and check out the anti-Semitism literature. I set the foul soup aside and headed toward the library to see what I could find.

# 22

# *Jewish Self-Hatred*

I t wasn't difficult to locate anti-Semitism in the library computer system. Titles like *If I Am Not for Myself* and *Living with Anti-semitism* popped up on the screen, directing me to the upper level library stacks. Following the numbers to the painful confrontation I sought, I was soon faced with an entire shelf of multicolored books. There was one called *With Friends Like These* and then, startlingly, a book simply titled *Jewish Self-Hatred*. This was something new: not just the prejudices of Christians against Jews. But Jews who hated themselves? I felt a shiver run down my spine. *"Not one of those Jews."* A little more than a month ago, I would not even have under-stood what there was wrong and hurtful about this response. I was only just now coming to realize the depth of alienation that these carefully chosen words revealed about me. For it wasn't only the Jews of the first century whom I thought of as "other." I was not one of the Jews who died in the Holocaust, who gesticulated with their hands, who took mikvahs, who played mahjong, who looked Jewish, who had social aspirations in Jewish circles, who participated in Hillel, who sent their children to Jewish summer camp, and so on and on and on. While my verbal deflections clearly satisfied my Christian conversation partners, my ready response did so at the expense of my religion, my people, and myself. Without being con-sciously aware of the fact, I had spent much of my life as a snag on the fabric of Christian anti-Semitism. I did not and arguably could not have had sufficient self-awareness to understand how fully and deeply I, a Jew, had integrated hostile and prejudiced attitudes about Judaism and Jews into my own psyche and spirit. As A.-J.'s course began to unravel loose ends of the pervasive Christian worldview, enhanced by the books on anti-Semitism and Jewish self-hatred I painfully consumed, it was as if I was following my Ariadne's thread. By pulling gently upon it, I felt myself led through a thicket of emotions ranging from embarrassment and intense anger to shame and excitement. Along the way, I was to be engaged critically with the New Testament, New Age spirituality, the Holocaust, and the future of our civilization. Most of all, however, I finally saw what many Jews have known for a long time. *Being a Jew in an anti-Semitic Christian world is tough.*

As I devoured the literature on the subject, turning it into research for my term paper with A.-J.'s permission, I came to understand that it is a temptation for more Jews than just myself to turn the intensity of negative feelings against certain aspects of our heritage, ourselves, and other Jews. It is a coping mechanism by which to avoid or minimize the pain. Often this is done on such an unconscious level, we do not even know we are doing so. That the issue of positive Jewish identification is a serious issue is paid mute testimony by these statistics:

- Between the French Revolution and World War II, hundreds of thousands of Jews converted to Christianity to overcome anti-Jewish hostility. On the eve of World War I, there were as many as 100,000 converts in Germany alone, alongside a Jewish population of 620,000.
- Among Jews by birth, only 11 percent of those who married before 1965 were married to somebody who was not born Jewish. This figure rose to 57 percent for those married after 1985.
- As of 1990, 59 percent of American Jewish households were unaffiliated with a temple or synagogue.
- As of 1995, 1.3 million adults and progeny of Jewish descent followed another religion, approximately equal to the same number of Jewish children killed by the Nazis.
- The global Jewish population, estimated at seventeen million prior to World War II, fifty years after the Holocaust, is still only thirteen million, four million shy of being replaced.
- Of the 770,000 children being raised in American interfaith households with one Jewish partner, 35 percent are being brought up with

no religion, 40 percent are being raised as Christians or in other non-Judaic religions, and 25 percent are being raised as religious Jews. The 25 percent of children of intermarried Jews being raised Judaically means that the future potential Jewish population is halved; 50 percent would be necessary just to maintain the status quo.

How many of these statistics reflect the understandable urges of deeply fearful Jews to protect themselves and their progeny from anti-Semitic hatred so pervasive as to be beyond rational or even conscious consideration? Until I was brought face to face with my deepest fears and suspicions during the course of my reading for A.-J.'s class, I was unaware of how much of my life was an unspoken response to having grown up in the shadow of the Holocaust. Perhaps I was not the only Jewish child who had sat before the images of skeletal bodies being flung into ditches, told by fearful parents that it was my lifelong duty to observe and remember. For years I had nightmares about piles of burning shoes blazing against the night sky. I stroked my own young, smooth skin as I watched strong-jawed Germans proudly displaying lampshades made of Jewish flesh. No, I was not one of those Jews. My distance could easily be explained further by the fact that I belonged to the first post-Holocaust generation. Born in 1948, I encountered my Judaism in a world in which the six million had already died and in which the state of Israel had just been founded. My generation entered a world in which the pain was so fresh and so great it was literally unspeakable. And yet, having all taken place before I was born, it seemed a world for which I bore no responsibility. Perhaps coping mechanisms were necessary, or at least understandable, given the cynical implications that could be drawn from the blue glow of skeletal images that flooded over us in our living rooms: *The Jews are helpless victims; there must be some reason why the Jews were singled out; there are better things to be than a Jew.*

As I was now for the first time seeking out literature addressing anti-Semitism, I had the sense that I was entering a new and largely unexplored world that mostly hints at rather than reveals the extent to which self-hatred has been behind the coping strategy for the many Jews of my generation, making our presence known to Judaism primarily as diminishing numbers on charts of Jewish statistics. For those of us who care about the ongoing existence and vitality of the Jewish people, Jewish self-hatred is a high-stakes issue that has to be addressed. The place where I began was to look at the pull of the Christian version of reality that so dominated the world of my childhood.

It's not that I'm not well-schooled in how much violence has been committed in the name of Jesus Christ. Of course there was the Inquisition; the bombings of Jewish community centers and synagogues; the job, social, education, and housing discrimination against Jews even in the community within which I was raised; the unwillingness of the pope to publicly decry the genocide of the Jews during World War II; and so on and on. But the Jesus I was introduced to as a child living in the Christian-dominated world of suburban America circa 1955 was as fun as Santa Claus, as loving as angels, and as good as God. While I knew that I was viewing Jesus as an outsider, I got the impression that the life of Jesus contained the elements that, in the words of Albert Schweitzer, "have evoked a response from all that is best in human nature. The Mother, the Child, and the bare manger; the lowly man, homeless and self-forgetful, with his message of peace, love, and sympathy."

What was there not to like? From bus posters to stained glass windows—everywhere I turned there were images of Jesus healing the sick, loving children, courageously dying for his beliefs on the omnipresent cross. And my Christian neighbors: how happy they looked opening Christmas presents, hunting for Easter eggs, all the while knowing that they were saved and going to heaven. As I grew from childhood into young adulthood, many in my generation grew out of fairy-tale versions of the life of Christ. But yet did "Christ-consciousness" remain as the ultimate New Age symbol of spiritual transformation.

But then there's the dark side, buried in my life. Overt in the lives of many Jews who suffered the taunts of their classmates, covert for the rest of us. "Jewish Self-hatred," a term first coined by Theodor Lessing in the Germany of the 1930s, "results from outsiders' acceptance of the image of themselves generated by their reference group—that group in society which they see as defining them as a reality."

Once the dominant Christian image has been accepted as the norm, the logical route to psychic (and perhaps even physical) self-protection is to dissociate one's own identification with the victim and seek refuge with the perpetrator. This urge can be subtle and unconscious, or conscious and literal. Theodor Herzl, before popularizing Zionism as the ultimate solution to "the Jewish problem," first proposed mass baptism of the Jewish people in order to spare their children the humiliation and danger of anti-Semitism.

The urge for self-protective dissociation is supported by the circumstantial evidence of popular culture. Christian holidays in America are largely celebrated as national holidays, with Easter passion narratives and Christmas nativity scenes dominating the media and the public square. Also celebrated are individuals whose anti-Semitism is well-known, such as Nathaniel Hawthorne, Herman Melville, Theodore Dreiser, Henry Adams, H. L. Mencken, Ezra Pound, T. S. Eliot, Charles A. Lindbergh, and yes, even Carl Jung and Joseph Campbell. Jews are submitted to a daily dose of columnists, speakers, flyers, and opinions by those who attribute their financial problems to Jewish greed, who ascribe the godless values in Hollywood and Washington to the secret agenda of a Jewish elite, the lack of unity and the delay of the Kingdom of God to the stubborn Jew in our midst. The "emancipated" Jew separates himself or herself as above or apart from the targets of anti-Semitism, often with serious ramifications. Karl Marx, who converted from Judaism to Christianity at the age of six, produced writings about Jews so vituperative that Adolf Hitler reported having gained some of his "insights" into Jews by reading them. American journalist Walter Lippman, when informed by Harvard president A. Lawrence Lowell of his intent to limit the "excessive" number of Jewish students at the university in the early 1920s, responded, "I do not regard the Jews as innocent victims. They hand on unconsciously and uncritically from one generation to another many distressing personal and social habits."

Another Jewish response to Christian anti-Semitism, well-disguised and rarely consciously apprehended, is the attempt by intellectually gifted Jews to raise the discussion to a higher level. Ruth Wisse writes: "To be sure, anti-Semitism has triggered tremendous bursts of energy in modern Jews. . . . Having no desire to engage their adversaries, they tried to prove themselves unworthy of hatred. . . . Just note the conspicuous role played by the 'Jewish question' in the search for universal theories of human behavior and in movements aimed at political redemption."

From Marx to Freud, from Franz Boas, the pioneer of anthropology, to Ludwig Zamenhoff, whose urge to create an international language was fueled by his desire to bring human beings closer together for mutual understanding: "In their own estimation these idealists were attempting to improve the condition of mankind as a whole, which is perforce a nobler ambition than merely securing the Jews," Wisse continues. "But the move into the embrace of mankind was a process of assimilation that would eliminate the Jews along with the need to defend them."

Regardless of how high-toned the mission, all of these Jewish responses have one common root. All have come into being within the dominant, anti-Semitic Christian environment. In writing about Henri Bergson and Simone Weil, French Jews who in affirming Christian spirituality repudiated the religion of their birth, Martin Buber explained that they had "turned away from a Judaism they did not know; in actual fact, they turned aside from a conventional conception of Judaism created by Christianity."

The place these Jews went to take refuge, identifying with the very reference group from which they needed greatest protection, was a place all too willing and adept at reframing Judaism and Jewish history in negative terms. Where Christian identification is high, statistics show that there are fewer Jews and their children attending temple or synagogue, reading the scriptures, understanding the tradition and teachings, reading and speaking Hebrew. The more detached the Jew becomes from his or her heritage, the less likely he or she is to feel identified with other Jews. As Robert Weltsch, Buber's disciple, noted in relation to the bourgeois circles of his youth, it was deemed tactless, or rather outright hostile, "for anyone to say he was a 'Jew.'" This reticence "was not simply opportunism. It also stemmed from a genuine embarrassment, engendered by an unclarity about what Judaism really meant. As the word *Jew*, emptied of all positive content, had shriveled up into a mere name of derision, it seemed only proper not to use it."

Jewish dissociation, then, is able to flourish in the pervasive environment created by Christian definitions of both Christianity (Jesus as evoking "all that is best in human nature") and Judaism ("the greedy, legalistic, pushy, conspiratorial ones who killed Jesus"). In order to hope to find a Judaism able to rise or fall on its own merits, the dissociated Jew must first make the Herculean effort to peel off the layers of Christian interpretation and environmental influences that diffract Jewish vision.

One place to begin is to raise the question of what contemporary historical critical research can tell us about "those Jews" who are accused of having opposed and killed Jesus Christ. As Jews gain access to this material through the hard, brilliant work of people like Professor A.-J. Levine, we will be in a better position to evaluate our relationship to our history and traditions, freed by contemporary scholarship from the filters of Christian anti-Semitism. Open-minded Christians, too, will benefit from a serious consideration of these questions, freshly armed with historical resources with which to combat the forces of anti-Semitism in their own congregations and culture. To begin this quest, the quest for the historical Jew, I turned my attention to the main source of Christian anti-Semitism and Jewish self-hatred, the New Testament.

# 23

# *Sacred Vituperation*

I had come to the Divinity School, I thought, in order to pick up some nice parables by Jesus to add to my collection of spiritual stories from many ages and traditions. Of course I was aware of the extremist Christian fringe that lapped at the edges of my social and intellectual enclaves. As winter began to give way to the first signs of spring, Jody and I treated ourselves to a dinner out at Boston Market in suburban Brentwood, near our home. My husband and son were off looking at colleges back East and Jody and I were discussing her recently announced plans to be Bat Mitzvahed in a couple of years. She was enjoying Congregation Micah, having made friends with a great group of fifth graders, many of them "just like me," one parent Jewish, the other converted or simply supportive. Feeling upbeat, we walked arm and arm out to our car for the short ride home. On the windshield, was a black and white pamphlet. It read, in huge letters, "HOPE FOR THE HOPELESS." I recognized it immediately as the same brochure Jered had shown me several months earlier, the day he'd told me about his dying congregant who ascribed her misfortune to Jews with horns. Legions of fervent churchgoers had made their way south, working shopping center parking lots in Tennessee just as, the month before, they had blanketed the state of Kentucky. Jody reached for it but I grabbed at it first. She didn't need to read: *The Lord's disciples knew the checkered history of the Jews well. They knew that God, on numerous occasions, had turned His back on them because of their sins and delivered them into the hands of their enemies.*

Before A.-J.'s course, I would have dismissed such verbiage as the product of a lunatic fringe of contemporary Christians, spinning delusional fantasies mostly out of their own sick imaginations. I knew that the mainstream interpretation of the New Testament ascribed the crucifixion of Jesus to the Jews, but beyond that I was ignorant as to what exactly the New Testament says on the subject. Ironically, it had never occurred to me that words as darkly drawn as these—and worse—about Jews and Judaism would have found their basis in the Christians' sacred text, itself. And not just in one place— the climax of the Passion narrative that I thought was told but one time in the New Testament—but over and over again in the multiple versions of the Passion, and laced throughout the Synoptic Gospels, John, Acts, and Paul. Through serious study in the contemporary historical critical tradition, the theological nuances and finer points of the anti-Jewish polemics begin to become somewhat differentiated into varying gradations of offensiveness. But overall, I was forced to admit that what I encountered in the pages of the New Testament exceeded my own worst fears and suspicions. No longer did I feel wonderment at the lunatic fringe of Christians who felt motivated to communicate their feelings on my windshield (and worse). Rather, I felt wonderment that based on the sentiments spelled out clearly and repeatedly in their sacred text, there are not more Christians who are following their lead.

Paula Fredriksen, in *From Jesus to Christ*, the book that A.-J. had given me to read and that served as a primary text in her course, details the many cases of anti-Jewish polemic, from temple cleansing episodes to theological debates, from betrayal to crucifixion, that occur throughout the New Testament.

> The Sadducees and Pharisees are a "brood of vipers" (Lk 3:7), hopeless hypocrites, whitewashed tombs that house uncleanness (Mt 23:27), murderers and persecutors of prophets and wise men. The Jewish followers of the Sadducean and Pharisaic leadership are not exempt from Matthew's invectives. Therefore as Pontius Pilate reluctantly leads Jesus before the Jewish accusers, the Jewish people scream out: "Let him be crucified . . . His blood be upon us and upon our children" (27:22–25).

Fredriksen points out that in the pages of the New Testement, Jews are portrayed as having rejected Jesus aggressively from the time of his birth (2:33ff). Says Fredriksen: In Matthew's estimation, "The Jews' treatment of Christianity is the ultimate expression of the 'law of history' whereby the Jews have always murdered God's prophets."

In the Acts of the Apostles, Luke characterizes Jews, in the words of Fredriksen, as an "ubiquitous lynch mob, murderously rejecting the good news of forgiveness and salvation . . . because they do not want to share salvation with the Gentiles" (13:16–52, 26:20–22). In Acts, three thousand Jews and proselytes are informed by Peter that Jesus "handed over to you according to the definite plan and foreknowledge of God, you crucified and killed . . ." (Acts 2:23). In John, the "Jews," in rejecting Jesus, reveal themselves to be "not of God" (9:47), having rejected the father, so earning "the wrath of God" (3:36). "Your accuser is Moses, on whom you have set your hope" (5:39). "He who hates me hates my Father also" (15:23).

Adding vivid color to the Jewish polemic is the portrait of Judas Iscariot. Rabbi Joseph Telushkin writes:

> Although Jesus and all his apostles were Jews, most Jews and Christians think of them as Christians. . . . The one apostle people naturally think of as Jewish is Judas. . . . As theologian Richard Rubenstein has noted, the lesson Christians learned was that no matter how close you think you are to a Jew, at the very moment the Jew is kissing you, he may be betraying you.

Because the issue at hand is related to money, the story adds fuel to anti-Semitic portrayals of Jews as greedy and opportunistic as well as devious and self-serving.

At the same time the New Testament provides anti-Semites with vituperative verbiage to use against the Jews, it undermines the possibility of mutual respect or peaceful coexistence by its insistent and repetitive contention that Jesus is the exclusive conduit to God. "For there is one God; there is also one mediator between God and humankind" (1 Tim. 2:5). There is "no other name" by which persons can be saved (Acts 4:1). Jesus is the "only begotten Son of God" (John 1:14). "I am the way, and the truth, and the life. No one comes to the Father except through me" (John 14:6). What took place in him was "once and for all" (Heb. 9:12).

It is common sense that this one-two punch of vituperative accusations and contentions could fuel anti-Semitic feelings among those exposed to them either directly or indirectly, from the parishioner in the pew to the self-studying zealot, from the bored hotel room guest randomly flipping open the Gideon Bible to the Jewish child seeing a crudely hand-lettered signboard held up behind first base at a nationally televised baseball game. But the anti-Jewish polemic of the New Testament does not affect only the uneducated, the fringe, or the anti-Semitically predisposed. Christian history pays bloody testimony to the fact that the verbiage lends itself to the justification of all manner of atrocities, not only against Jews but also against non-Christians of many ages and cultures, not to mention Christians of divergent denominations or traditions.

Many contemporary Evangelicals, far from seeing the words of the New Testament as an impediment to the creation of environments in which anti-Semitism thrives, see them as a call to support such environments. In a significant gathering of Evangelicals held in Lausanne, Switzerland, in 1974—Billy Graham's International Congress on World Evangelization—2,470 representatives of 150 countries and 135 Protestant denominations affirmed "the absolute authority of the Bible, the uniqueness of Christ, and therefore the pressing need for evangelism. Because Jesus is the only God-man, because he is the only mediator between God and man," the Congress rejected "any kind of syncretism and dialogue that implies that Christ speaks equally through all religions and ideologies." Expressly denied was any possibility of salvation through other religions.

While the anti-Semitism fed by the New Testament can be blatant and overt, it is not only the obvious and unselfconscious adoption of denigrating points of view that affects those living in an environment dominated by Christianity. As I had encountered in my studies of Jewish self-hatred, the urge of the Jewish minority to protect itself from the pain of being identified as "the enemy of God" compounds proactive anti-Semitism with the potential for reactive dissociation. But it is not just Jews who seek protection from such invective. Sensitive liberal Christians, who identify strongly with Christianity as a religion based on love of one's neighbor, in keeping with the highest moral and spiritual ideals, also find themselves in the uncomfortable position of protecting themselves from dissonant aspects of their own scripture and tradition that would otherwise, if directly confronted, prove unacceptable or at least unsettling to them.

In my observation of many of my divinity school classmates, I discovered that such protection was made possible by (and requires) an enormous investment in denial. This denial appeared to be accomplished by a combination of factors. The most prominent of these factors falls under the general category of "fogginess." This fogginess appeared to be institutional, personal, or a combination of both. My liberal Christian classmates explained their diffuse sense of never before having "gotten" the anti-Jewish polemics in the New Testament. Other classmates pinned their fogginess on churches that "picked and chose passages carefully," avoiding controversial or dissonant text, or minimizing scripture entirely, relying instead on self-help type sermons and approaches, such as positive thinking or spiritual healing.

But as the semester unrolled, even as I began to wake up from my long winter's nap, so my many Christian classmates roused themselves to awareness and dismay, struggling to break the denials and rationalizations in which they sought protection from the spiritual and moral dissonances of their tradition. Happily, among the students were many sent by their denominations with the explicit purpose of courageously confronting the mythologies surrounding their own sacred text, willing to struggle head-on with the moral and spiritual discrepancies in both historical and theological contexts. These Christian academics and church leaders stand beside their Jewish colleagues, as well as courageous scholars from other faith traditions, in what I believe to be the key task for religion in the twenty-first century. Given the volatile nature of the subject matter in question, the stakes are enormous for individuals at virtually all points on the philosophical and theological continuum. Those who pioneered the field during the nineteenth century, such as David Friedrich Strauss and Bruno Bauer, put their careers and lives on the line for their intellectual freedom. Albert Schweitzer wrote: "The critical study of the life of Jesus has been for theology a school of honesty. The world had never seen before, and will never see again, a struggle for truth so full of pain and renunciation as that of which the Lives of Jesus of the last hundred years contain the cryptic record."

And what do historical scholars now think was the reality of the core conflict between Jesus and "the Jews"? Fredriksen is one of many historians who have analyzed every moment of Jesus' story, looking for discrepancies, anachronisms, hearsay, mistakes, translation problems, misinformation, unfounded contentions, mythic layering, prejudicial theological and political agendas, and other signs pointing toward historic improbability. Under the scholars' scrutiny, the nature and/or existence of the relationship of John the Baptist and Jesus, the mission and the message of Jesus, the composition of the twelve disciples, Jesus' entry into Jerusalem, the temple-cleansing incident, the last supper, the arrest and trials of Jesus, the role of the Jews in his crucifixion, the role of Pontius Pilate and the Romans, and the resurrection itself—are all put into question.

As the semester unfolded, of greatest interest to me was how unstable and unreliable the historical basis was for Christian anti-Semitic sentiments—and, therefore, of that degree of Jewish self-hatred which derived from the majority point of view. In other words, the coping strategy of choice for many Jews—the viewing of those Jews who opposed Jesus as being "other"—is predicated on a Christian construction built upon a faulty historical foundation. The real issue for contemporary Jews is not how different (better) today's Jews are from "those Jews," but, rather, how can we reclaim our own history and see "those Jews" through Jewish eyes freed from the filters of Christian dogma, prejudices, and tradition? At the same time, we need to make a sincere effort to familiarize ourselves with our own tradition. By doing so, alienated modern Jews would be freed from the consciously or more often unconsciously held feelings of shame, alienation, and estrangement that turned us against ourselves, our religion, and our tradition and that have manifested themselves in falling statistics.

# 24

## *Those Jews*

So what is the truth about the Jews of the first century? There's one thing we know for sure. The Jews back then, as now, were not perfect—not morally, spiritually, or socially. Then again, they were and are no worse than any other diverse group of individuals who, upon the great surprise of finding themselves in human bodies, must do their best to come to terms with their fellow human beings, the traditions and environment to which they are born, suffering and mortality, and the meaning of life.

But back in the first century, was there a particularly sinful generation of Jewish leadership? While the New Testament portrays Jesus predicting total destruction of the Jerusalem Temple as punishment for their faithlessness, for murdering their prophets, and for turning their backs on God—"Truly, I say to you, there will not be left here one stone upon another, that will not be thrown down" (Matt. 24:2; Luke 21:6)—do we know that the Temple leaders were really as faithless as they are portrayed?

Jacob Neusner, in his book *Judaism in the Beginning of Christianity,* addresses the popular conception among both Jews and Christians that the generation of Jews that populated the world of Jesus and his contemporaries was a sinning one:

> It was not a sinning generation, but one deeply faithful to the covenant and to the Scripture that set forth its terms, perhaps more so than many who have since condemned it. . . . On what grounds are they to be judged sinners? The Temple was destroyed, but it was destroyed because of a brave and courageous, if hopeless, war. That

war was waged not for the glory of a king or for the aggrandizement of a people, but in the hope that at its successful conclusion, pagan rule would be extirpated from the holy land. . . . It was a war fought explicitly for the sake and in the name of God.

Neusner goes on to point out that the Jerusalemites fought with "amazing courage, despite unbelievable odds. Since they lost, later generations looked for their sin, for none could believe that the omnipotent God would permit his Temple to be destroyed for no reason." The God of the Jews expects much of us. Throughout our long history, Jews have been taught that it is our sole purpose for being alive to rise to God's occasion. Looking at turning points in Jewish history, it becomes clear that with the destruction of each temple, and, in fact, on the occasion of just about every blow from fate, Jews willingly take on the yoke of believing themselves to be exiled in punishment for their sins. But this prophetic self-flagellation is not to be taken as proof that the Jews in question are particularly sinful by objective standards. It is an indication of a prophetic perfectionism by which many Jews measure themselves and their fellow Jews against their ideals.

So if that generation of Jews was not particularly sinful, what could explain the New Testament's vituperative attribution of such negative qualities to the Jews in relation to Jesus? This is a deeply complex question and I realized that to answer it completely would take me many more years of study. In any case, before taking this question on in even a preliminary way, I must raise yet another yellow—if not red—flag. For one must be careful not to assume that such antipathy between Jesus and the Jews did in fact exist, thereby confining one's scholarly inquiry as to the cause. There is, in fact, conflicting evidence as to if and whether the tension between Jesus and the Jews existed, and if it did of what it consisted.

According to Fredriksen, the central explanation given by most New Testament scholars has been "to locate that offense in Jesus' supposed attitude toward the Law. Since Jesus both forgave sins and taught on his own authority, this explanation goes, he essentially announced in his person and ministry that the authority of the Law had come to an end. . . . Jews hearing such a message, Jesus knew, would naturally kill the messenger. . . ."

After a thorough consideration of both the New Testament passages and what scholars can agree upon concerning the historical context, Fredriksen summarizes:

> If Jesus during his ministry had abrogated the Torah, apparently neither his own disciples nor Paul himself knew. . . . Paul says repeatedly that the source of his Law-free gospel was not human tradition but his vision of the Risen Christ. It is difficult, then, to sustain the position that Jesus during his lifetime publicly taught against the Torah, and thus that such teachings were a source of mortal conflict between him and his contemporaries. . . . It is difficult to find a source of religious conflict between Jesus and his Jewish contemporaries.

Fredriksen goes on to tackle the second major issue raised by scholars as an explanation of tension between Jesus and the Jews: Jesus' teaching that God was loving and merciful, forgiving repentant sinners, preferring mercy to sacrifice. Far from offending his Jewish audiences to the point of murderous retribution, this message of mercy and forgiveness is entirely consistent with Jewish scriptures and tradition. Flip open the Hebrew Scriptures to just about any of the Psalms. Psalm 55, for example:

> As for me, I will call upon God;
> And the LORD will save me.
> Evening, and morning, and at noonday, will I complain, and moan;
> And He hath heard my voice.
> He hath redeemed my soul in peace so that none came nigh me . . .

Another question worth asking is this: If the conflict between Jesus and the Jews was so great in the first century, why isn't there more of it in Jewish writings and oral traditions of the time? The authors of the New Testament portray the Jews as obsessively concerned with the life and death of Jesus. However, noting that the majority of rabbinic writings, including the entire body of the Talmud and the Midrash, post-date Jesus as well as the New Testament, it is startling that an event so volatile and noteworthy as the alleged Jewish crucifixion of someone thought by some to be the son of God should receive so little attention in Jewish testimony. What is the explanation for this apparent lack of interest among the post–New Testament Jewish writers? One possibility that has been suggested is that the Jews may well have not been overly concerned with attacking Jesus and with continuing hostilities against the early Christians simply because they were so busy going about their real business, that is, engaging actively in the practice of Judaism. Morris Goldstein in *Jesus in the Jewish Tradition* writes:

> Judaism, in its unfolding during the first centuries of the Christian Era, had its own problems of survival and its own evolving message for guiding and enriching the life of the Jewish People. Its teachers, therefore, engaged in a very minimum of discussion concerning Jesus. The positive side seems to have been emphasized, not the negative. The rabbis, in the main, did not set out to demonstrate what was wrong in the teaching, claims or acts of Jesus and his disciples but rather to stress what was good in the Jewish tradition.

The question remains as to what was on the minds of the authors of the New Testament as they penned their so often vitriolic condemnations? The general consensus among the historical Jesus scholars I studied is that the real opposition to Jesus came not from his fellow Jews, but from Rome. This Roman tension was an antipathy that increased rather than lessened between the time of Jesus' ministry and the writing of the New Testament. Many of the scholars cited demonstrate in great detail the vested interest the New Testament authors had at the end of the first century in putting the blame for Jesus' death on the Jews and deflecting heat from the Christians' tenuous relationship to Rome. Pointing out that the more the New Testament tradition evolves, the worse the portrayal of the Jews becomes, Fredriksen explains that following the war of 66–70, the period in which the Gospel accounts as well as particularly bitter Pauline passages were composed:

> The church had every reason to want to assure prospective Gentile audiences that the Christian movement neither threatened nor challenged imperial sovereignty the way the Jewish people had, despite the fact that their founder had himself been crucified, that is, executed as a rebel. . . . The danger of even seeming to stand in political defiance of Rome was too great, the potential price too high.

The Christians of that early era established an unfortunate tradition for those times throughout history when anything goes wrong: blame the Jews.

Raising these uncomfortable issues is not meant to diminish the significance and truth of Jesus in relation to believing Christians. As Maurice Friedman, student and interpreter of Martin Buber, writes, "the innermost reality of a religion, its all-holiest and all-realest, is only accessible to the consecrated." To the degree that Christians experience Jesus as their conduit to God, transforming their lives according to the highest moral and spiritual ideals of their faith, Jesus and Christianity bear witness to uncontestable (if not exclusive) spiritual truth.

That Christianity can rise to the occasion of supporting the Jewish task of the reclaiming of our faith and history from the shadow of Christian anti-Semitism, is testified to by the courage and honesty of some Christians in their relations to Jews throughout time.

In 1963, shortly before his death, Pope John XXIII composed this prayer in atonement for the Church's history of anti-Semitism:

> We realize now that many, many centuries of blindness have dimmed our eyes, so that we no longer see the beauty of Thy Chosen People and no longer recognize in their faces the features of our first-born brothers. We realize that our brows are branded with the mark of Cain. Centuries long has Abel lain in blood and tears, because we had forgotten Thy love. Forgive us the curse which we injustly laid on the name of the Jews. Forgive us that, with our curse, we crucified Thee a second time.

As a result of my studies both in the classroom of Professor A.-J. Levine and as I read the literature on anti-Semitism, I no longer saw those Jews who killed Jesus Christ as "other." When I began my study, I had a hunch that this might prove to be the case. What I did not expect was that I would also reclaim my relationship to contemporary Jews and Judaism, recognizing compassionately beyond the veils of Christian interpretation, the single wellspring from which we Jews have understandably drawn different life experiences. I no longer saw the Jews of my parents' generation (including the victims of the Holocaust) nor of my own generation as "other," either.

But perhaps most remarkably, and unexpectedly, I glimpsed a vision of what I believe to be the truth: that at that same wellspring, drawing nourishment from the very same spiritual source—sharing the God of Abraham, Isaac, and Jacob, Sarah, Rebecca, and Rachel—are Christians past, present, and future. Perhaps there is hope of a time when Jews will no longer see Christians as "other" and Christians will no longer see Jews as "other," as well.

In the words of Heschel, "Holiness is not the monopoly of any particular religion or tradition. Wherever a deed is done in accord with the will of God, wherever a thought of man is directed toward Him, there is the holy."

# 25

# *Jered's Sermon*

My involvement with the anti-Semitic research preoccupied me for much of the semester. While in process, I was too raw—too vulnerable—to share with my classmates. Willow, Emma, and Lester seemed similarly preoccupied with their own personal as well as scholastic agendas as the costs of a theological education that Dean Fitzmier had warned us about at our opening day's luncheon an eternity ago began to take their toll. With Sammy gone, his whereabouts still unreported, we were losing the sense of being fellow campers. Often, I found myself in the library instead of at coffee hour. I sat alone at lunch, open books surrounding me. At night, my studies took precedence over board games and television. I often turned my back to Jody, directing her to her dad for attention as I worked against the increasing demands of assignment deadlines. The only lifeline I had to the Div School community was the prayer group, that had continued meeting once a week despite Sammy's poignant absence and our harried schedules.

I looked forward to the group as the one place I knew I could go to vent my feelings. Early in the semester, I arrived in a terrible state, having come directly from Buttrick's class where Jered had just given his first sermon on the class theme: "What does it mean when I speak the word of God?" It had been dreadful: a saccharine exhortation to his congregants to pray for the Jews *"because they aren't all bad."*

"Jesus taught us to take care of the weak and the misguided. The leper, the prostitute, the poorest among us. Should we be any less generous in our time and age than Jesus was two thousand years ago? I don't think so. There are amongst us those who for whatever reason have not heard the Good News. They are not to be condemned, but loved. For they, too, are God's beloved. When I speak the word of God, the word is love. I am learning to love those whom others despise. I am reaching out to those who are different from me offering the gift of peace and understanding. I trust that it will be out of my love, not my fear or my hatred, that I will be doing my part to hasten the second coming of Christ. We must never give up hope that ears will open, eyes suddenly see. And then, we will no longer have our differences between us. We will all know the Truth. And the Truth is what Jesus Christ died for us to know: all you need is love. Because the Jews can not and will not pray to Jesus for themselves, it is our task as Christians to hold the faith for them. In the name of Jesus Christ, our Lord and Savior. Amen."

The sermon was hard enough for me to take, but the fact that it had taken place just a week after my sour soup lunch, when I had failed to respond to Jered's "compliment" that I wasn't like "those other Jews" filled me with guilt. Obviously, Jered had taken my silence that day to mean that he was on the right track. The struggle seemed overwhelming, as I needed to sort through my own mixed feelings about Judaism while simultaneously devising a strategy to take on the misconceptions of those around me. Jered had actually turned to me after the sermon, winking broadly as if he had just given me a great gift. By his simple gesture, I felt doubly condemned.

As the semester unrolled, each of us in the group struggled with our demons. Every one of us had sunk down into the mire where individual spiritual work demanded our serious engagement. Lester's financial, familial, and vocational problems were worsening to the point of crisis. His wife had given him a six-month warning. If he did not land an academic position by the new year, he would have to return to full-time work in the ministry, a calling from which he had been feeling increasingly alienated. Clearly, Lester did not like surrendering control of his own destiny—neither to his wife, nor to God. He was doing his part, everything he could, to follow what he believed to be God's voice, calling him to go in a new direction. But Lester could not make the phone ring, the letter of a job offer arrive.

While he sermonized week after week about God's mercy and the wisdom of faith, Lester was deeply distressed by his own fears that God was letting him down. We empathized with Lester, understanding uncomfortably the discrepancy between professing a rich, deep relationship with God when things are going our way and feeling abandoned when things are not. "Fair-weather faith," we called it. Over and over again, we prayed for a faith strong enough to sustain us during bad times, as well as good.

We prayed just such a prayer for Emma, who took turns crying about missing her children and problems with her ordination. What should she do? None of us could answer that question for her. She huddled endlessly with the other women in the school who were in the same boat. She meditated and prayed and began seeing one of the Vanderbilt therapists. We held her hands, feeling helpless as we witnessed her relentless struggle. Only Willow presented a cheery front, proceeding with her plans to convert to Catholicism. While she presented the most upbeat stories week after week, in many ways she seemed the most fragile of the group. But, in truth, we all seemed fragile.

It was late in the semester now—a moment of particular tension for the student body as deadlines for papers collided with take-home exams and in-class presentations. I'm sure that each one of us contemplated skipping prayer group just this once, in order to use our most precious resource—an hour of time—to hack away at our growing burdens. The idea of finishing all of my assignments on time, in respectable fashion, was becoming more and more remote. I imagined that Willow, who on top of this semester's responsibilities still had the task of tidying up last semester's incompletes, was even more beleaguered. Would she show? In fact, while I got to group on time, I was the only one who managed. Lester had failed to come early, as was his practice, to set up the chairs. Vaguely, I wondered if anybody really was going to bother to come, when suddenly my friend Carlton, the army chaplin in training who had driven me crazy with questions about mikvahs, burst into the room.

"My God," he cried. "There's been a suicide."

"A suicide? Who?"

"I don't know. I just know it's one of the first year students. That's all they're saying. Isn't it horrible? Who would do such a thing?"

The empty chairs stared at me ominously. Who, indeed?

Carlton ran on, the town crier, leaving me alone in the vacant room for too long. As I sat, I thought about each of my friends. We were all under incredible pressure—but suicide? I closed my eyes in prayer: please God, let Willow and Lester and Emma be all right. And Sammy! I shuddered as a chill went down my spin. Was it Sammy? "Did you hear?" It was Lester. Thank God, Lester was all right, but, I reminded myself, he was not a first year student.

"Are they saying who?"

"No."

Lester sat next to me and we held hands. Again the wait was interminable. And then, after many long moments, I heard voices in the hall. Women's voices: Willow and Emma. And so all the seats were soon filled but Sammy's. We sat together in silent prayer. What could one say? I was relieved it wasn't any one of us, but I dreaded hearing the news about who it was. Out of the corner of my eye, I saw Willow fingering her rosary beads. A single, simple desire began to formulate in my mind. I needed to speak with Rabbi Kanter.

As I drove up West End Avenue to Congregation Micah, I tried to formulate what it was I would be asking for. In the few months since we had joined, Congregation Micah had proven to be a positive addition to our lives. Both Grant and Jody had made new friends, friends that they did not have to explain or defend themselves to. The community had welcomed us with open arms, and Dan and I began to have personal exchanges with many of the people who came regularly to Friday night services. As we attended several of the other social events—a trip to a baseball game with the family, a visit to a comedy club with adults only—we saw the potential for this eclectic group of Jews—and the people of other faiths who loved them—to become a new kind of extended family. Amazingly enough, we had even begun to recognize the temple melodies. In fact, I often caught the temple's catchy version of the Sh'ma, which had originally caused me such discomfort, meandering through my mind. What had once seemed foreign and strange those first weeks was becoming familiar. The rabbi offered a number of classes that looked fascinating, classes on the prophets, and the Talmud, but busy as I was with my class-work, I had not yet been able to attend. And in any case, it had become suddenly clear to me that I had a need: an ache in my heart that education had only seemed to worsen. With all that I was receiving, yet I wanted—no, I needed—something specific from Judaism, something I had not yet gotten.

Rabbi Kanter motioned to me to sit down while he finished the call he was on. It was a journalist asking him about the vision for the human rights commission he was heading up for Metro Nashville. And then we talked. We discussed the guilt I felt over having failed to respond to Jered. I told him about the suicide and my fear that I had somehow failed the Div School community. The heartfelt words Rabbi Kanter comforted me with, crafted by his lifelong involvement with Judaism, rang true and clear. We talked about the prophet Micah and Ecclesiastes and Job. And yet I still needed something more. But what? Then suddenly, even as the realization of what it was I was looking for was freshly breaking over me, I spoke my unedited thoughts out loud.

"A ritual. Some kind of spiritual experience. I don't know. Forgiveness. The Kabbalah, maybe. Isn't there something in the Kabbalah that might help?"

"I don't know," Rabbi Kanter responded kindly but firmly. "I'm not familiar with the Kabbalah."

"Well, something. Jewish meditation. Dancing. I don't know. Something!"

"I don't dance. Look, Carol, you're still trying to make us into your Marin County Shabbos Shul. We're not that."

"But we could be."

"Is that what you really want?"

I thought of the ephemeral nature of the Shabbos Shul community, the peaks of ecstatic spirituality separated by wells of loneliness.

"Not exactly. I like what we've created here. But can't we do something, something spiritual to touch and heal those places in us that would otherwise not be reached? I understand now that Friday night services, the Sabbath, is not the time for breast-beating. But I need time, more than once a year, for giving vent to my feelings. Surely there are others of us in our congregation who are hurting. Must we wait until Yom Kippur to beg forgiveness?"

After a long pause, Rabbi Kanter finally replied: "I hear you and I understand what you're looking for. I'm just not sure I can give it to you. But I'll make a deal with you. The Jewish Community Center is looking for some representatives from Micah to go through a leadership training program. I'd like to give them your name. When they call you, would you seriously consider doing the program, to see if there might be some way for you to make a contribution to the community—share your vision, bring about the changes you hope to see? Meanwhile, I'm going to think about what you've said. Okay?"

On the long ride back home, I found myself thinking about another rabbi in my life, Rabbi Siskin. For three decades, I had silently accused him of forsaking God for politics: Why was it that I had been forced to get my spiritual juice from Buddhist chants and Zen meditations when there was a rich spiritual vein to mine within my own tradition? If it hadn't been for my spiritual explorations in other cultures and traditions, I wouldn't even have known what to ask for. I now knew that spiritual ritual was, indeed, a part of the Jewish tradition. Where had it gone? Politics? But as I now re-ran old tapes in my mind, I recognized the possibility that Siskin's response to the troubled times of my youth may well have been to steer a steady course through routines which, in themselves, may have rung hollow to many ears. Imagine the burden on the Reform rabbis of the early 1950s—leading Friday night services, weddings and Bar Mitzvahs, even while footage of the Holocaust was being shown to American Jews on television for the first time. Working out of a prayer book and theories from a more innocent era, he had the formidable task of leading his flock to some sense of meaning and purpose at a time when many of the leading Jewish thinkers of his time were busily declaring that "God is dead." Placing his emphasis on the politics, growth, and development of Israel, as God's answer to Auschwitz, now makes more sense to me than it did at the time. But was there more to the story than that? Why was it that the Reform Judaism within which I was raised so consistently left some deep part of me—some mystical/spiritual potential I now know to be part of the tradition—untouched?

I thought of a favorite story I had encountered while preparing my paper on anti-Semitism. The story was told by Reb Zalman, who described his father as a spirited *shaliach tzibur*, leader of prayer.

*One day, Papa is under the tallis and I hear him crying.*
*"Papa," I say. "Why are you crying? Who hit you?"*
*Papa responds, "I was talking to God."*
*I ask, "Does it hurt when you talk to God?"*
*"No, it doesn't hurt when you talk to God; you're just sad that you waited so long since talking to God."*

That was how I felt: tears for what I so sorely missed, but in my case, had never had. I fully believed now that my birthright had been a deep, personal, emotional relationship with God within the Jewish tradition. What had gone wrong?

In Zalman's culture—the Eastern European shtetl Jews, from whom I, along with the majority of Jews in this country, hail—such effusions of faith were the norm rather than the exception. Many of the ghetto Jews of Russia, Poland, and the surrounding areas brought with them to this country a hearty, personal relationship with God. In the great wave of immigration that transplanted the residents of entire villages to cities like New York and Chicago in the decades before and after the turn of the century, the Jews managed to import their emotionally involved relationship to God—working against tremendous social and economic pressures—establishing multiple shuls on nearly every block of their transplanted shtetls.

Meanwhile, forces were at work in the Jewish community in America, as they were in Eastern Europe, to temper and quell the hearty spirituality not only of Hassidic and ghetto Jews, but of all recent immigrants. This suppression, which was to largely succeed, was but the latest effort in a long history of class-based struggles in the American Jewish community designed to suppress overt spiritual expression. Even as I prepared my final papers, I broke open a whole new literature, concentrating on the history of Jews in America, and began to read.

# 26

# *Passion and Prejudice*

The Eastern European Jews were relatively late arrivals to this country. Preceding them were several waves of immigrants, beginning as early as the seventeenth and eighteenth centuries. Among the earliest of the Jewish arrivals were Sephardic Jews from Spain and Portugal. Few in numbers, hailing largely from the educated, upper-crust of Western Europe, they quickly formed a Sephardic aristocracy in America. They adhered to an austere Orthodoxy, a far cry from the overtly emotional and mystical spiritual practices of the Jews who would soon arrive to their shores. This next group, the second wave of immigrants, consisted of German Jews. Unlike the Sephardim, who were primarily merchants, the German Jews were mostly peddlars and the like. However, lower-class Germans were not the only Jews to arrive in this first mass migration. Arriving, too, in the 1800s, were educated Jews who brought with them the principles of the Enlightenment, embodied in Reform Judaism.

Long before their arrival to our shores, the intellectual German Jewish elite had embraced the philosophy of the Enlightenment as a way out of anti-Semitism's focus on the particularity of the Jew. Struggling against the anti-Semitism of the European academic community, as well as in European society in general, German Jews such as Moses Mendelssohn realized that Christian peers formed their image of Jews primarily out of their interactions with the poorer Jewish peddlars they saw selling their wares at trade fairs. The German Jewish intellectuals went on the defensive to prove that Jewish culture was not the primitive, lower form of religion these poorer Jews appeared to be practicing. To defend the contemporary value of his tradition, Mendelssohn felt compelled to draw a hard line between the defensible rational basis of Jewish philosophy and practice and the lower-class culture that caused him so much embarrassment. To accomplish this, the emotional, spiritual, and mystical aspects of the folk tradition were dismissed by the Jewish intellectuals as nonsense, superstition, and fanaticism.

With the philosophers of the Enlightenment providing the intellectual rationale for the suppression of emotional and spiritual expression, many of the newly arrived Jews who aspired to become established in America felt compelled to minimize those aspects of their religious and communal life that differed from the mainstream's Anglo–Saxon code of decorum. As the Germans quickly learned to suppress their visible ethnicity in favor of social mobility, they took their place beside the Sephardim, making manners and refinement their cultural ideals. It was into this decorous climate that the third wave of Jews, the nearly two million Jews from Eastern Europe who came to America between 1880 and 1920, arrived. Having learned the lesson of economic and social mobility to be gained by assimilation from the Sephardim, the German Jews, while overwhelmed by the huge numbers of Eastern European Jews who flooded into their cities, rose to the challenge of "Americanizing" the new immigrants as they had been Americanized themselves.

Among their greatest challenges was to rid the new arrivals of their "embarrassing" mannerisms, putting in place of their effusive ghetto expressiveness the American virtue of fitting in. The German Jews, concerned that the visibility of the new immigrants would inspire a rise in anti-Semitism, were hypercritical of their differences. In 1903, Rabbi William Friedman declared: "We, who are the cultured and refined, constitute the minority [but we] shall be judged by the majority, by the Russian Jews, by the children of the Ghetto." Chapters of the Jewish charitable organization, B'nai Brith, found the new immigrants too vulgar and uncivilized for membership. "More polish, less Polish" was the motto of one such chapter. But they did want to help. Among the German Jews' strategies was the distribution of etiquette books and the establishment of settlement houses and classes to teach the new Americans manners reflecting the mainstream's emphasis on self-discipline, order, and control. The public schools also took a leading role in the Americanization of the immigrants—not just Jews, but children of all cultures and faiths. (In order to teach them not to gesticulate with their hands, young Italians in New York City were instructed to sit on their hands at school, for example.)

While many of the Eastern European immigrants felt liberated by the Enlightenment's universalizing tenets (my grandmother Rebecca, among them), and grateful for the assistance they were receiving from those who came before them on the road to becoming "modern" Americans, the class issues between cultures and philosophies were bound to erupt. Where they erupted primarily was in the struggle for control of the religious life of Jews in America. The 1800s, with the rise to prominence of the Enlightenment's form of Reform Judaism, inspired furious exchanges between those who proposed to emphasize the rational aspects of Judaism, and Orthodox and Hassidic rabbis who fought to preserve traditional, spiritual, and folk expressions of the religion. While such disagreements resulted in the permanent split of American Judaism into separate branches, the dominance of Reform was also the triumph of rationalism. "Be no fanatic. . . . Be intelligent and allow your reason to govern your passions, propensities, and superstitions" was the watchword of the Reform Jewish philosophy.

In the face of the Enlightenment, Judaism needed new models for American Jewish worship. Dr. Isaac Mayer Wise, father of the Reform Jewish movement, admittedly performed radical surgery on the Jewish tradition "in order to save the patient." The spiritual, emotional worship of the Orthodox Jew was "updated" in order to be "made more respectable for Jews themselves and for the outside world." Traditional Jewish religious costumes and practices, including the warmth and energy of the disorderly medley of praying voices expressing their living, emotional relationship to God as practiced in the shuls of my father's childhood, were discarded. Jews, who had wandered freely about the synagogue floor, were now confined to pews. Formerly chaotic prayer rituals were harnessed into responsive reading, moments of silence, and listening to sermons. Where the rabbis once prided themselves on their Talmudic scholarship, this very credential was perceived by many "modern Jews" as being superfluous or old-fashioned. In its place, rabbis were encouraged to obtain a general university education. Religious practice as a whole moved toward the secular, with many Reform temples becoming more like community centers than spiritually charged halls of worship.

Just as class and economic pressures contributed to the urge to minimize differences between Jews and the Christian mainstream, so did the division of Judaism into branches reflect class and economic stratification. Orthodoxy and shtetl values were a burden on those who aspired to social and economic acceptance by the mainstream, prerequisites for advancement in society and work. As the Eastern European Jews and their children advanced economically and socially, they increasingly left behind the Orthodox traditions to adopt the Germans' Reform or Conservative forms of Judaism. All this brings me to ask what I believe is a key question for contemporary American Jews: Why is it that mystical, spiritual experience, in life and in worship, is considered by many Jews—including many in leadership positions—to be a lesser expression of Judaism?

Some indication as to what this prejudice is about may be exposed by the fields of sexual psychology and politics, where "emotionality" is suggested to be the surface manifestation of what those in power truly fear: loss of control. We have already discussed the fact that when Jews suppress their emotional and mystical expressiveness, they often take on—consciously or unconsciously—the decorum of the Christian mainstream. Interestingly enough, Robert Goss, in his book *Jesus Acting Up,* explains contemporary scholarship's understanding that the early Christian church feared sexual impulse as the most powerful competitor for human loyalty. He sees the urge to desexualize the masses in the development of Christian imagery. A virgin birth, a celibate Christ, a disembodied Holy Spirit: these images positioned the Christian mainstream away from early Judaism's hearty celebration of the goodness and fecundity of embodied creation and toward the Hellenic ideal of neutralized sexuality. Sex became associated with sin, evil, and the devil, because it was only by satanizing sex that the church could hope to keep absolute control.

The Jewish Enlightenment, while not focusing specifically or consciously on sex, was equally concerned with elevating order and control to a position superior to the irrationality of spirituality. As Wise exhorted his fellow Jews to "allow your reason to govern your passions," one can not help but notice that there were others who judged the emotional expression of Jews as a primitive, inferior religious and cultural form. The darkest expression of this tendency became visible in the polemics surrounding the movement toward federal legislation to restrict immigration from Southeastern European countries that ultimately succeeded in their goal in the early 1920s. Proponents of restriction argued that "the country was sliding downhill because of racial deterioration. The unrestricted invasion of Jews, Italians and Slavs, the beaten breeds, would eventually outbreed their superiors." While the issue of emotion in the Jewish worship on the surface, seems simply a matter of taste, class, or philosophy, the implications in relation to the darker aspects of the human potential for death and destruction are chilling. There are those who, for whatever reason, fear the power of emotion, and the emotionally charged religion and culture of first generation Jews reflected the very cultural particularity their children sought to suppress. To act on this fear, particularly as it relates to the implications of sexual suppression, is to wish annihilation on a people. Simultaneously, for Jews—or anyone—to surrender the right to natural, emotional experience and communication, particularly in an area as intimate as one's relationship to God, is to allow one's self to be controlled by other people's agendas. It can be, taken to its logical consequences, even a matter of life and death. One of the primary values of the German Nazi's master race was "gentlemanliness."

The price of resistance to this call to suppression can be high, but there is a price, too, for compliance. Just as Italian schoolchildren were taught to sit on their hands, non-Orthodox Jews have been taught to sit quietly in their pews. Whatever emotion managed to seep through to my generation of Reform Jews arrived in the form of a sentimental nostalgia for the way things used to be. Jews, as well as Christians, can rent the video of *Fiddler on the Roof* and vicariously imagine, for a few hours, what true religious fervor must have felt like. But it can not be denied that there is a huge hole in contemporary American Judaism. Where the "uncouth" immigrants once roamed vital and free, their hearts and spirits were intact even if their pockets were empty and their days numbered. I propose that today, the lack of vitality credited in part to the modern suppression of emotional expression and mystical experience, can be witnessed statistically in our diminishing numbers. But, despite the urgency of the issue, there is cause for optimism.

Rebounding from our largely spiritually arid childhoods, the urge among my generation of Jews to have a rich, expressive relationship with a reality greater than ourselves and to create a vital, living Judaism can not be denied. Those among us who instinctively yearn for a personal relationship with God, but who cannot return to the restrictive religious laws and trappings that our parents discarded for us, have felt ourselves to be exiled from our true spiritual home.

As I rode home from the rabbi's chambers that spring day, still suffering painfully in my concern over who it was that our class had lost to suicide, I suddenly realized that the anger I had felt for so many years toward Judaism had gently subsided. I was disappointed that Congregation Micah did not have a mystically evocative spiritual component in place, but I also understood the hard work the Reform Jews had already undertaken, freeing themselves from arcane and burdensome aspects of the tradition that needed to go. I am thankful that through the efforts of Reform Judaism I was granted social and economic benefits and did not have to suffer the limitations my Grandma Rebecca endured in her Russian shtetl. My ability to think and to question, my feminist sensibilities, were all nurtured within the fresh air of the Reform Judaism of my childhood. However, the time has come to counterbalance the modern excesses of rationalism in order to retrieve the emotionally expressive spiritual core that has been part of Judaism since David swooned in ecstasy before his God.

I remember Lester's warnings about the emotional excesses of New Age spirituality, misguided individuals who believe themselves to be in direct communication with the Divine, unmediated by any intellectual or rational component whatsoever. But to throw out the experiences many of us who passed our adolescence in the New Age have had with the Divine simply because they were not authorized by an institution is to throw the baby out with the bathwater. The next step for many of us is to test out our history and potential for spiritual experience within the framework of our tradition. As 1 Kings 22—the lying spirit of King Ahab's time—reminds us, there are no guarantees that when we open ourselves to dialogue with the Divine, we won't be misguided, make mistakes, and maybe even worse. With stories like the lying spirit of the Book of Kings, our tradition teaches us that to be Jewish and to dream of worshipping God with one's whole mind, spirit, and heart is a high-risk business. I believe it to be a risk worth taking.

# 27

## *Finals*

The first year student who commited suicide was somebody I did not know, neither by name nor by face. It wasn't one of the public wrestlers: screamers, criers, strugglers, who thrashed about in the underbelly of theological emotion, painfully but inexorably filling in the God-shaped void with hard-won meaning. People like Willow and Lester, Emma and me. And it wasn't Sammy, either, although he had yet to be heard from. The individual who commited suicide was somebody who had been a stranger to me, his anguish private, personal, and silent. Rumors circulated about the cause, but who really knows? I felt the loss terribly—we all did—as any family would who lost one of its own. I struggled with the news, and with feelings of my own guilt for having somehow fallen short as part of a community that fails to take care of its members. But just as much, the news reopened questions that I had only begun to explore concerning God's role and responsibility in the midst of life's tragedies. While I had come some distance with Heschel's concept of God, with the news of the suicide—and all of the questions it raised for me both theologically and personally—I knew I had a ways to go.

I carried around the book on process theology that Lester had told me about, but it would be two more years before I would find the time to read and understand it, incorporating it finally into my life in such a way as to bring me the peace of mind I was on the way to finding. But the days rolled on into the last week of classes before finals, as trees viewed mostly through the streaked glass of classroom windows blossomed. We had to switch the time for group that week to accommodate Lester's fitting for his graduation robes. But after the suicide it had seemed particularly important to reach out to one another and make the effort to stay connected.

Having already been through one round of finals, I knew that there would be no sense of completion for our little community other than what we could accomplish today. There would be Lester's graduation, of course. But many of us, including myself, would not be there, having been called by our various causes and obligations to other parts of the country and world. We would take our finals, quietly leaving the blue books on the front desk, wandering out of the building and into the next phase of our lives with nary a wave or a hug. Knowing this, today had taken on added meaning.

Lester lit a candle, as was our ritual week after week for the many months we had been praying together, setting it in the center of our circle. We sat in silence for many long moments, holding hands and feeling each other's presence in the bonded community we had become. Knowing that this was the last time we would all be together, I felt the pain of separation in equal proportion to the poignancy of how much I had grown in the presence of this rare gathering of individuals of varying ages, races, and religions. The I Ching explains relationship like this: it is the one who knows the greatest love who is capable of experiencing the greatest pain. This is the double-edged sword of real relationship. Is this a curse or a blessing? On this important point, the I Ching refuses to pass judgment. It is up to the individual alone to make up his or her mind on this point. As I looked around at the dimly lit faces, flickering in the diminishing candle's flame, I knew that whatever pain the relationship of community brings in its wake, I could no longer have it any other way.

Lester went first. He had received incredible news, he whispered. An assistant professorship at his denomination's seminary had been offered to him. A decent salary, housing, and medical benefits. No longer would he have to balance four jobs, school, and home responsibilities.

"I'm kind of embarrassed to admit it," he said quietly. "But I believe that it's entirely possible that my vocational jitters were nothing more than fear. Now that I've got the job, I realize that I knew all along that God was calling me away from church ministry and into the academy. I just wish we could live our lives in retrospect. It would be so much easier to have faith then! Anyway, that's one of the key areas I will be working on at the academy: the issue of discernment."

On this side of the notification, Lester realized that all the sacrifices had, indeed, been worth it. Not only was he going to continue to be a minister of God, but he would be on a track within the institution where he could begin to influence policy and theology for his denomination as a whole.

Emma also had good news.

"The judge just ruled that the children can spend the whole summer with me! They're arriving next week!"

And she had finally made up her mind about ordination.

"I've prayed and journaled and meditated and talked to God—with a few therapists thrown in along the way. And I know what I must do. I've decided to take my denomination's terms, distasteful though they are. I realize that I've got a better chance of changing the institution from the inside than if I opted to go it alone. I hope you guys will pray for me. You've been my backbone through this darkest of semesters. And now, it is such a blessing to finally see the light! How can I ever thank you all?"

The calmness of her demeanor informed us without words that this was not a resignation, but acceptance. The hum of gratitude and appreciation, while expressed in silence, filled the room with light.

We could have sat quietly together for many more moments, basking in Emma and Lester's joy, but it soon became obvious that Willow had something important to say.

"I'm going back to South America for the summer. I found a program, and it's perfect!"

It wasn't Catholic, Jewish, or even Episcopalian, but a social services project sponsored by an independently funded citizens group. It would mean an interruption in her conversion process, an interruption that she had come to believe was for the best.

"Roman Catholicism on the rebound from a mugging is not the kind of theological commitment the priest had been hoping for," she explained.

"He and I think that a summer's contemplation is called for at this point. Maybe it's not a good idea to take on new institutional commitments while still in the middle of Div School. It's only been one year. Just think how much more I'll know in two or three more years! I need to let this year's experiences sink in deeper, to go slower and open myself to receiving God's guidance, instead of shopping around for a religion like a bargain-hunter after Christmas."

It felt right and good. I was so excited for Willow, Lester, and Emma, each of their lives shifting on the axis of their faith and hard work to a new, higher center. Even though Lester was to move to another state, he promised to come visit—and I knew he would. And Emma and Willow? We had years and years together in which to grow and nurture our friendships. But now it was my turn. How should I spend my five minutes? What of the many thoughts and feelings, challenges and accomplishments that I had behind and ahead of me, should I share? There was nothing big—a job offer, a summer in South America, the return of my kids and the decision to go for ordination. But one piece of news emerged from the rich fabric of what my life was becoming that begged to be told.

"I decided to get on a committee with the Jewish Community Center."

"You did?" The group exclaimed, knowing how far a journey such a destination as this had entailed. "What will you be doing?"

"I'm going to help them with membership. There must be a whole lot of Jews like me who somehow slipped through the nets and are looking for a way back in."

"A fisher for souls?" Willow asked, impishly.

"No fair mixing metaphors!" I replied, knowing that Willow was alluding to Jesus. In an instant, any sense of betrayal I had felt dissipated in the love that passed between us. Was Willow a Jew, a Roman Catholic, an Episcopalian, or an Apostate? Who cared? Ultimately, there was something more important to be said. Willow was my friend.

As the hour neared completion, we stood in a circle, holding hands, reluctant to release the physical grasp of the community we had become: a community that understood that while each of us hailed from different religious traditions, there was a power greater than any institutional expression—a unity, a divinity—that did not belong to any one of us, but to all of us together. If only Lester weren't leaving, all of us going our separate ways for the summer and then in two or three years, to missions, churches, and writing assignments around the country and the world. What would it be like if this level of spiritual and emotional intimacy were possible on an ongoing basis? That would be a religious institution I would want to be part of!

We left each other with hugs and tears. And while the prayer group was now over for me for the semester, my schoolwork was not. I had A.-J.'s final examination to go. And then there was my last sermon for Buttrick's class: "What I Mean When I Say I Speak the Word of God."

Ironically, Jered's final sermon was to take place on the same day. A few days before our presentations, he stopped me in the hall.

"Carol, you've got to help me."

"What's the problem?" Jered's face was redder than usual, and he was short of breath.

"I'm so scared of saying something unintentionally anti-Semitic, I've got total writer's block. Look at this!" He opened up his notebook to a page full of scratch-outs. You see, unlike the time months ago when he'd spoken out of turn in Barr's class to silent response, when he'd given his sermon in Buttrick's class—his well-meaning but misguided offer to save the Jews—it hadn't been me who took him on. The whole class pounced on him, lecturing him on Christian imperialism, egocentrism, intolerance, and the like. Now he was terrified of a repeat performance.

"If I cite one of the New Testament passages that puts down the Jews, I'll have to spend the whole sermon apologizing for my tradition. I'll never get to anything inspirational or positive for my congregants. If I avoid all the theologically debatable passages, discussing the implications, contexts, and limitations, they'll get an education, but they won't get spiritual guidance. If I say God is male, the women will jump on me. I don't know where to begin."

"Why don't you begin with what's in your heart?"

"What's in my heart is that despite all of this, I know that Jesus loves me."

"Okay. Say that."

"You're telling me to say that?"

"What's wrong with that?"

"Oh, I don't know. Maybe just two semesters of getting bashed on the head for being insensitive or something."

"Jered, there's a huge difference between claiming exclusivity—diminishing other people's religious and spiritual choices—and having faith in your own relationship to God."

"Jesus."

"Okay, Jesus."

"You don't have a problem with my belief that Jesus died for my sins and that the Kingdom of God is coming?"

"Look, Jered, it's not what you believe—it's who and how you act in the world that I care about. Didn't Jesus say 'by their fruits they shall be known?' I love what Rabbi Heschel said about religion. He wrote that a religion should be judged not on the basis of the worst that comes of it, but the best. I would have to say, getting to know you this year, that you are courageous, sincere, loving, even the kind of person Jesus hoped you would be."

"But I thought you hated all this Jesus stuff."

"I never said that. I admit that ultimately God is a deep mystery to me. Who knows what is really true? We have our traditions to guide us, but we both know that our traditions aren't foolproof. And so we do the best we can, working with the systems that we've been born into, using our hearts and our minds to critique those elements that no longer serve us, coming to new and better understandings through our communication with the Divine. Isn't that what the Holy Spirit is all about?"

"I've got it," Jered exclaimed. "I'll do my sermon about the Holy Spirit." He ran off, a few scribbled pieces of paper flying loose from his notebook as he headed for the library.

# 28

## *God's Word*

As I headed for Buttrick's class, I found myself stopping every
few steps to fix one word or another of my sermon. While I
was very interested in what Jered had to say during his final
sermon, to tell the truth, I was preoccupied with my own upcoming
presentation. As Jered stood before the class at the podium, I heard
enough to realize that he had found a way into his material that did
not take prisoners from other religions down with it.

"I can not deny the reality of Jesus in my life. At a time when I
was lost in the world, Jesus came to me and turned me from my self-
destructive ways and toward a higher purpose. When I say I speak the
word of God, I aspire to give voice to the spirit in me that resonates
with the teachings of Jesus. But even more than the words that I use
is the way that I act in the world. I experience in my relationship with
Jesus the divine spark of God urging me—urging all of us—to be better than we have yet shown ourselves to be. I have tried to act in a way
worthy of the one who came to teach us to love not only thy neighbor,
but thine enemy. It isn't always easy. Even when I try my hardest, still
do I often fall short of my goals. But when I stumble, Jesus is there to
catch me. This is the spiritual journey that Christians are invited to
embark upon through Jesus Christ. What peace I have found for
myself, I wish for you, as well. In the name of Jesus Christ, my Savior
and my friend. Amen."

At the conclusion, Buttrick joined the class in praise of his hard-
won progress. Jered's was a potent faith, sure of Jesus' love and
empowered by Jesus' message. His progress over the year exemplified
the best of what Rabbi Heschel once said, in "No Religion Is an

Island," his landmark speech on interfaith relations, delivered at Union Theological Seminary in 1966.

> I suggest that the most significant basis for meeting individuals of different religious traditions is the level of fear and trembling, of humility and contrition, where our individual moments of faith are mere waves in the endless ocean of mankind's reaching out for God, where all formulations and articulations appear as understatements, where our souls are swept away by the awareness of the urgency of answering God's commandment.

I believe that every religion is a particular response to a historical apprehension of Divine Reality. We must each take our community's own symbols seriously, using them as a portal into the mystery. At the same time, I believe both Judaism and Christianity would be well-served to recognize that we are each groping toward an enhanced relationship to ultimate concerns greater than that which can be contained exclusively within any one human institution. I agree with Heschel who instructs us that what is peculiar to each is not what is most essential to each:

> The supreme issue is not the Halachah for the Jew or the Church for the Christian—but the premise underlying both religions, namely, whether there is a pathos, a divine reality concerned with the destiny of humanity, which mysteriously impinges upon history; the supreme issue is whether we are alive or dead to the challenge and the expectation of the living God.

To be alive to the challenges of the living God means to be willing to set aside one's preconceived notions of not only one's own faith but also another's in order to grapple with the difficult and dissonant aspects of each and all. One does so in hope that through the confusion and struggle, beyond our dogmatic understandings of Jesus and God, will be experienced moment by moment the luminous integrity of Ultimate Goodness. This is not to say that we adopt a milquetoast universality in which the disagreements are glossed over and the lifeblood of one's faith trivialized. Rather, such work requires the participation in mutually respectful dialogue where all representatives are genuinely willing to peel away the layers of human frailty, limitation, and destructiveness that can dim the core of divine experience that resides in the bosom of every faith. As Heschel instructs us, the goal is to destroy the shallowness of religion, not their identities. I am encouraged that a new generation of Christian theologians and Jewish thinkers are engaging in this process at places like Vanderbilt Divinity School, in a spirit of mutual respect, trusting that as we do so, we increase the likelihood of being gifted with moments of apprehension consistent with the best promised by both Judaism and Christianity.

Over the course of the year, Jered realized that he could have and share his relationship to God and Jesus with others without having to make other religions wrong along the way. As praise heaped upon praise, Jered was beaming with delight. And then it was my turn. I looked around at my classmates, feeling the nervousness subside as I took in their supportive eyes, realizing that despite my great fears at the beginning of the year, my self-consciousness at being the only Jew in our class, they were sincerely eager to hear what I had to say. I cleared my throat and began to read:

"Recently, I awoke from a disturbing dream with a question formulating in my mind. There had been a series of nonmemorable occasions in the week preceding, in which I had felt called upon to give more of myself to my friends and associates than I was likely to receive in return. Simultaneously, I had just finished reading Viktor Frankl's work based on his experiences in the Holocaust, *Man's Search for Meaning*. The moments of self-sacrificing love depicted in his book were brutally few and far between, precious though they were. I was particularly disturbed by Frankl's observation that in the camps, to keep one's self alive, one was often compelled to satisfy one's physical needs at the expense of others. "*The best of us did not survive,*" he wrote.

"As I prepared to greet the day, I was suddenly swept with an overwhelming sense of self-pity for all the sacrifices I've made in the name of God. Had my generosity, my charity, my reaching out to others in love merely made me weak—easy to take advantage of? Why did it always seem that it was on my shoulders to give of myself to others while others so often felt apparently so little obligation to offer the same in return? And then, as I sank deeper and deeper into a familiar hole I've been in too often before, I realized that my very human emotions had dug so painfully deep, they had exposed a fundamental question that begged a response. It is, I believe, the question that all true religion poses to us. *Do I really believe that there exists for me and the universe a loving God—or not?*

"To reply in the negative would justify my sinking deeper into despair. On the other hand, I know from experience that, whatever it might cost me, the only way up and out of the abyss would be to find a *yes*. Feeling the darkness closing in on me, I leaped for the *yes* as if it were a rope thrown by God's very essence to me. For me, there is no alternative but to take the leap that life has purpose, that self-sacrifice has meaning, that the Divine calls to me and to us for some greater good than we may be ever able to grasp. This is the very essence of what I think of when I refer to God. It is a transformed experience of being alive that causes me to transcend my own self-interest in taking the risk of believing that it is worthwhile to love others, to sacrifice for others even knowing that in doing so one becomes vulnerable, exposes one's self to pain and the potential for disappointment. As I had the opportunity later in the day to finish reading Frankl's book, I grasped that he was one who faced this question in the most desperate of circumstances—and yet found it within himself to grab the rope over and over again.

"So what does it mean to me when I say that I have been called to speak the word of God? There is a terror to this, an audacity, that causes me to speak and write knowing all the while that at its very core, the act, itself—let alone the cause and result of one's faith—defies words and descriptions. There are those moments when I have been touched so deeply—by an act of kindness, by beauty, by pain—that the retelling of it re-creates the time, the place, the circumstance with which my readers or listeners may identify. Words artfully chosen can inspire listeners spontaneously to transcend their own finite boundaries to taste the possibility that there are unseen powers greater than themselves acting in their lives and in the universe. Stories can evoke the central spiritual act as if it happened to them. We intuit that the word of God has been spoken when the speaker and those who are fully present to the truth being communicated find themselves to be more rather than less willing to grasp the rope.

"But more often, I have found that it is not my eloquence nor my narrative abilities, but rather, my wordlessness, my helplessness, my finitude that most surely elicits an evocative resonance in others. For in truth, the essence itself defies description—can not be spoken. In this case, it is not the direct naming of God but rather, the stripping away of superficial names and understandings of God that opens an empty space within which we are sometimes, somehow, gifted with an experience of God's presence. We use words to strip away our false understandings of the universe, and of God, until we are left standing painfully naked—but perhaps closer to the Truth—than we had been before.

"We begin speaking the word of God when we become willing to be truth-tellers—to unveil our weighty idolatries, to warn against our nihilistic tendencies, to strip away our false understandings of God and of meaning down to the barest bone. We must become willing to struggle with the big questions, to huddle naked and alone in the shadow of the mystery; to submit our fondest notions, theological and otherwise, to scrutiny; to survey the literature, spiritual and religious, for the words of others who bring forth in us the resonance of truth. We must find it within ourselves to sit quiet, empty, waiting for as long as it takes for one real word truly worth speaking to rise to the surface.

"Having said all this, I am ready at last to turn my attention to my relationship to what it means to speak the word of God within my own tradition, Judaism. However it was, by fate or willfulness, I was raised in a childhood religious tradition that did not seem to encompass everything I felt God was guiding me to take on. During my prolonged adolescence I did not rest long within any philosophical system, always feeling the boundaries pressing hard in on me. By all accounts, my life would have been simpler had I joined my many peers in secular pursuit. Why could not God die for me, rather than lodging firmly within my heart and spirit, forcing me not only along the road less traveled, but often where there was no road at all? And then somehow, within the directionless chaos of rejected notions and defrocked teachers, to have found a voice true enough to have become a beacon for myself from within my own tradition! How mysterious are God's ways.

"Since I have been attending classes at Vanderbilt, I have become increasingly comfortable with the idea of reclaiming the religion of my birth—Judaism—understanding, as I now do, how much room there can be within liberal mainstream religions to struggle with issues, raise questions, and experiment with new interpretations. The Judaism I am encountering at Vanderbilt—and through my new affiliation, Congregation Micah—is large enough to encompass all that I am. I am committed to helping people see that a thoughtful, sincere willingness to struggle with spiritual and ethical issues is the heeding of God's word, more so than a superficial and untested adoption of biblical truth or any other doctrine.

"I was thrilled earlier this semester, when researching a paper on the prophetic role in Judaism, to have encountered something in the Jewish tradition called a *maggid*. The maggid is one who, while not a rabbi, is yet called to speak the word of God. In medieval times, up through twentieth-century Europe, they would travel from village to village sharing their simple stories with all who would gather. Self-ordained, they knew that God was speaking through them, substantiated by the fact that people showed up to listen and were transformed for the better by the encounter.

"It is in the spirit of the maggid that I stand before you, believing that what I am sharing with you is God's word. And what is that word? The word is *yes*."

And so it was that I left my last class of the semester, exhausted by the effort but certain that coming to Vanderbilt—investing the time, the energy, and the spirit—had more than offset the costs of a theological education. As pleased as I was with my performance, I felt a sense of bittersweet sadness that, with the exception of A.-J.'s final, the year had ended. I would miss my friends, the teachers, the classes over the summer. And once again, I worried about Sammy. Was he all right? Would I ever hear from him again?

As I pulled into my driveway, I reached into the mailbox, gathering up the phone bills and advertisments I knew would be inside. But there was much, much more. For among the handful of envelopes was a postcard from San Francisco: a shiny green, blue, and orange photograph of the Golden Gate Bridge. It was a postcard from Sammy!

> Hello Berkeley!
> Ran away from home—none too soon.
> Entering law school here in September on scholarship.
>
> All my love,
> Sammy.

But the postcard from Sammy wasn't the only surprise.

Nestled on top of the handful of bills was a folded cream-colored flyer, sent to our family from Congregation Micah.

Spiritual healing service.
Sundown next Saturday.
Edwin Warner Park. By the river.

# 29

## *Yes*

On an unseasonably cold Saturday afternoon, a group of forty Jews huddled together in a circle, shivering in the cool breezes of spring. Facing one another, we listened as Rabbi Kanter recited psalms. Our cantorial soloist, accompanied by Dan and several other congregants, played guitar and flute quietly in the background. And then something revolutionary happened. One among us began to weep. Soon there were many moist eyes as the spirit of the circle moved us to compassion and empathy. We felt connected. We felt whole. We felt forgiven. There was no question for any of us in that circle that day: God was among us.

What made this simple, sweet event revolutionary—as well as sacred—is that spiritual emotion was not just allowed to emerge from the congregants, but actually encouraged. This conscious inclusion of emotion, at the expense of control and rationality, signaled to me that issues related to class, theology, and anti-Semitism had quietly turned a corner toward resolution.

What was strikingly important about this group of Jews is that we were not standing outside the mainstream of Judaism, disenfranchised from institutional life. We were gathered together under the auspices of our institution. We were reciting psalms, not mantras, feeling the power of our own tradition's liturgy when shared in a communal context. With the single tears that rolled down many of our cheeks, we were taking the first tentative step toward the reintegration of an emotionally grounded relationship with a living God back into our lives and worship. I saw in that circle the beginning of a recovery from the shock of Holocaust with its desperate although understandable God-is-dead theology. I saw in it the full-circle arrival of Sephardic, German, and Russian Jews feeling secure enough in our economic and social progress to allow ourselves to let our guard down in public, in a group, as Jews. I saw the confidence of a community, stable enough to embrace the non-Jews in our midst: spouses and friends who cared enough about us, about the tradition, to want to participate and support an authentic Jewish life. I saw in it a rabbi, trained in the Reform tradition, willing to stand with us shoulder to shoulder, allowing spirit to move us, trusting that in walking this new ground together, the congregation would grow together rather than fall apart. Most of all, I experienced first-hand the magnificent potential of the Jewish tradition to transform both ourselves as individual Jews and our religious institutions, to make the effort consciously to renew our sacred covenant—a living relationship with our God.

I was home.

# POSTSCRIPT

In February of 1997, several months before receiving my Masters of Theological Studies degree, on the day of my forty-ninth birthday, a regular mammogram showed up evidence of breast cancer. As I embarked on a series of operations and procedures, I continued to work on this manuscript, the basis of which formed my senior project. I believe this book to be the most important of my works to date, and it was interesting to me that in the simplification of life—and clarification of priorities—that occurs when faced with a life-threatening disease, taking care of myself and my family and completing this book emerged as my top priorities.

I could not keep up with my community involvements during this period. But the number of calls I had to make to resign this or that committee or board let me see first-hand just how involved and committed I had become to communal life—Jewish, interfaith, and otherwise—since my first year at the Divinity School. Rabbi Kanter had been right. The focus on self-fulfillment and the search for peace, which had fueled so much of my past several decades, benefited greatly from balance with the more traditional Jewish emphasis on serving the community through charitable involvements.

While I did not expect recognition to come as a result of my service, the outpouring of support and affection for me and my family during this troubled moment was and continues to be astonishing. Between Congregation Micah, the Div School, Penuel Ridge Retreat Center, and the Jewish Community Center (not to mention from Dan's friends in the music industry), we had offers for as many as three dinners a night. In my recovery and treatment, Willow and Emma have been regular visitors, the three of us improvising together rich, wonderful healing services and rituals drawing from a variety of traditions, as our friendships continue to grow. Lester and Marvin both graduated with honors and are long gone to their academic posts, along with Sammy, who by all reports is doing wonderfully well at law school. They are often in my thoughts and prayers. I am no longer lonely for community. In fact, if anything, I am overwhelmed!

Last year, Grant was part of Congregation Micah's first confirmation class, eleven teenagers knitting together into a tight and loving group, actively supporting one another through several tough situations including our own family's current challenge. Jody is now training intensively and enthusiastically for her fall Bat Mitzvah. Congregation Micah recently moved from the former discotheque into its new building, an inspiring temple where I can definitely report that God is fully present. Dan has been asked to play guitar and sing Jewish folk songs with some of our fellow congregants at an upcoming Micah dedication ceremony, a privilege to which he readily acceded.

And for me, I discovered that my time at the Divinity School had been more than well spent, in particular when it came to working out my relationship with God. While the full working through of the relationship took every bit of the three years since that New Students' Luncheon an eternity ago, there did come a time when I had asked every difficult question of God. Of particular help to me was my encounter with process theology, which I'd heard about from Lester my first year, but didn't have the opportunity to dig into seriously until my third year under the tutelage of Professor Sally McFague and her brilliant teaching assistant, Emily Askew. By the time I was facing issues of my own mortality, I felt only that God was with me. Issues of inappropriately assigned blame and anger had already been resolved. Throughout my three years at school, and the several recent months of this illness, I have stayed in close contact with Professors Buttrick and Levine. Professor Buttrick, in the twilight of his long, productive career is finally, reluctantly, facing retirement. Vanderbilt will suffer a great loss when he leaves. Professor Levine, in the heat of her career, is emerging as an academic superstar, with an endowed chair, alongside an increasing résumé of honors and appointments. If you haven't heard of her already, you soon will.

As for me, when I walk across that stage at Vanderbilt's Benton Chapel to get my diploma this May—bald head under my tassel and cap—I will relish the words Dean Fitzmier promised to speak to us on this important occasion: *"There walks a theologian."* Placing my trust in God, I believe myself to be at a new beginning, not an end. The very day I had to tell people in my divinity school community that I was going for surgery was the day the school secretary handed me my letter of acceptance into the Doctoral program at Vanderbilt in the area of Historical and Critical Theory of Religion—Jewish Studies focus. My prognosis for recovery from the breast cancer is excellent. And so it is that I make plans to embark on my doctorate this fall. My goal is not to become either the most knowledgeable Jew in the world nor the most pious. Rather, I hope only — as a result of my growing relationship with God — to be a better Jew than I would otherwise have been.

Because I did so much work on Jewish theology subsequent to the year described in this book, I have already begun work on my next book about my Jewish journey: a systematically worked-through accounting of my understanding of my religious tradition. I hope you will find it interesting.

Until then, with deep love and respect, Shalom.

Carol Matzkin Orsborn  
Nashville, Tennessee  
Spring 1997

# FOR FURTHER STUDY

*During the course of my Masters, I read hundreds of books—each of which made a contribution to my return from exile. In addition to the many books mentioned in passing throughout this book, the following are books that I found to be particularly influential in my own journey back to Judaism.*

## BOOKS THAT HELPED ME FEEL LESS ALONE IN MY UNCONVENTIONAL SEARCH FOR GOD

Boorstein, Sylvia. *That's Funny, You Don't Look Buddhist*. San Francisco: HarperSanFrancisco, 1997.

Goldman, Ari L. *The Search for God at Harvard*. New York: Ballantine Books, 1991.

Heschel, Abraham Joshua. *A Passion for Truth*. Woodstock, Vt.: Jewish Lights, 1995.

*The Holy Scriptures*. Philadelphia: The Jewish Publication Society of America, 1917.

Kamenetz, Roger. *Stalking Elijah: Adventures with Today's Jewish Mystical Masters*. San Francisco: HarperSanFrancisco, 1997.

## BOOKS THAT FANNED THE FLAME OF JUDAISM IN MY SOUL

Citron, Sterna. *Why the Baal Shem Tov Laughed: Fifty-Two Stories about Our Great Chasidic Rabbis*. Northvale, N.J.: Jason Aronson, 1993.

Kamenetz, Roger. *The Jew in the Lotus*. San Francisco: Harper SanFrancisco, 1995.

Kushner, Harold S. *To Life! A Celebration of Jewish Being and Thinking*. New York: Warner Books, 1993.

Anything by Sholom Alechem.

BOOKS THAT ENABLED ME TO SEE THE ANTI-SEMITIC
WATER EVEN ASSIMILATED AMERICAN JEWS SWIM IN

Fredriksen, Paula. *From Jesus to Christ*. New Haven: Yale University
Press, 1988
Gilman, Sander. *Jewish Self-Hatred*. Baltimore: Johns Hopkins
University Press, 1986.
Reinharz, Jehuda, ed. *Living with Antisemitism*. London: Brandeis
University, 1987.

BOOKS THAT HELPED ME GET AN ADULT HANDLE ON THE
JEWISH TRADITION THROUGH CONTEMPORARY TIMES

Dorff, Elliot N., and Louis E. Newman. *Contemporary Jewish Ethics
and Morality: A Reader*. New York: Oxford University Press, 1995.
Katz, Steven T., ed. *Interpreters of Judaism in the Late Twentieth
Century*. Washington, D.C.: B'nai Brith Books, 1993.
Telushkin, Joseph. *Jewish Literacy*. New York: William Morrow, 1991.

BOOKS THAT GUIDED ME TO REALIZE THAT THE JUDAISM I
COULD BE RETURNING TO WAS NOT THE UNDERSTANDING
OF JUDAISM I LEFT BEHIND

Cooper, David A. *Renewing Your Soul: A Guided Retreat for the Sabbath
and Other Days of Rest*. San Francisco: HarperSanFrancisco, 1995.
Dosick, Wayne. *Dancing With God: Everyday Steps to Jewish Spiritual
Renewal*. San Francisco: HarperSanFrancisco, 1997.
Heschel, Susannah, ed. *On Being a Jewish Feminist: A Reader*. New
York: Schocken Books, 1983.
Hoffman, Edward. *The Heavenly Ladder: The Jewish Guide to Inner
Growth*. San Francisco: HarperSanFrancisco, 1985.
Lerner, Michael. *Jewish Renewal*. New York: Harper Perennial, 1994.

BOOKS THAT REMIND US THAT STRUGGLING TOWARD
UNDERSTANDING BETWEEN RELIGIONS IS NO LESS
THAN WHAT GOD EXPECTS OF US

Harrelson, Walter. *Jews and Christians: A Troubled Family*. Nashville: Abingdon Press, 1990.
Kasimow, Harold. *No Religion Is an Island: Abraham Joshua Heschel and Interreligious Dialogue*. Maryknoll, N.Y.: Orbis Books, 1991.
James, William. *The Varieties of Religious Experience*. New York: Macmillan, 1961.

BOOKS THAT DEEPENED MY RELATIONSHIP WITH GOD

Frankl, Viktor. *Man's Search for Meaning*. Boston: Beacon Press, 1962.
Heschel, Abraham Joshua. *I Asked for Wonder*. New York: Scribner, 1954.
Heschel, Abraham Joshua. *Man's Quest for God*. New York: Charles Scribner, 1954.
Heschel, Abraham Joshua. *God in Search of Man*. New York: Farrar, Straus & Cudahy, 1955.
Lubarsky, Sandra, and David Ray Griffin. *Jewish Theology and Process Thought*. Albany: State University of New York Press, 1996.

OTHER BOOKS BY CAROL (MATZKIN) ORSBORN INCLUDE

*Solved by Sunset: How to Solve Whatever's Bothering You in One Day or Less* (Harmony Books)
*The Art of Resilience: One Hundred Paths to Wisdom and Strength in an Uncertain World* (Three Rivers Press)

Carol Matzkin Orsborn is available for speeches and workshops. To contact her, send e-mail to CORSBORN@AOL. Her website address is: www.MSBN.com/carolorsborn.